Classic Pin-Ups Grayscale Adult Coloring Book

Compiled by Renee Davenport

Cover Colorist Nina D'aloia

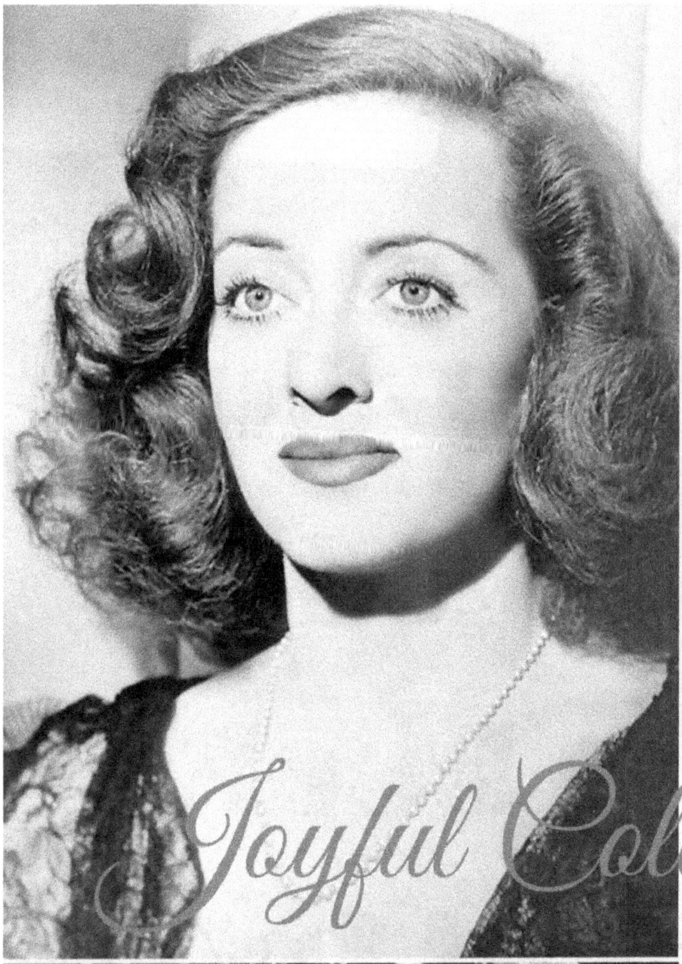
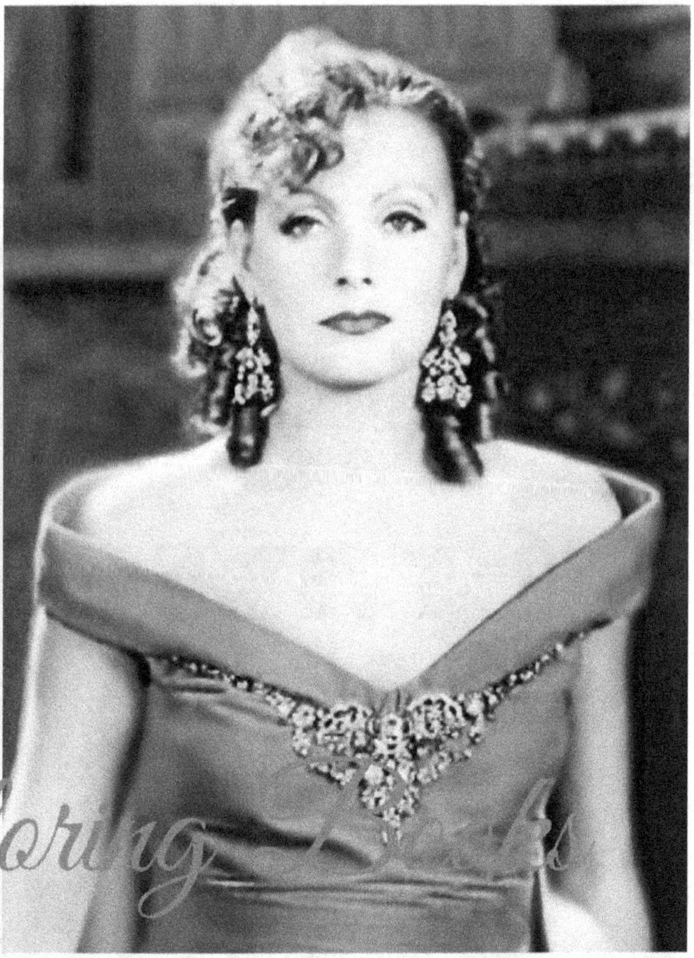

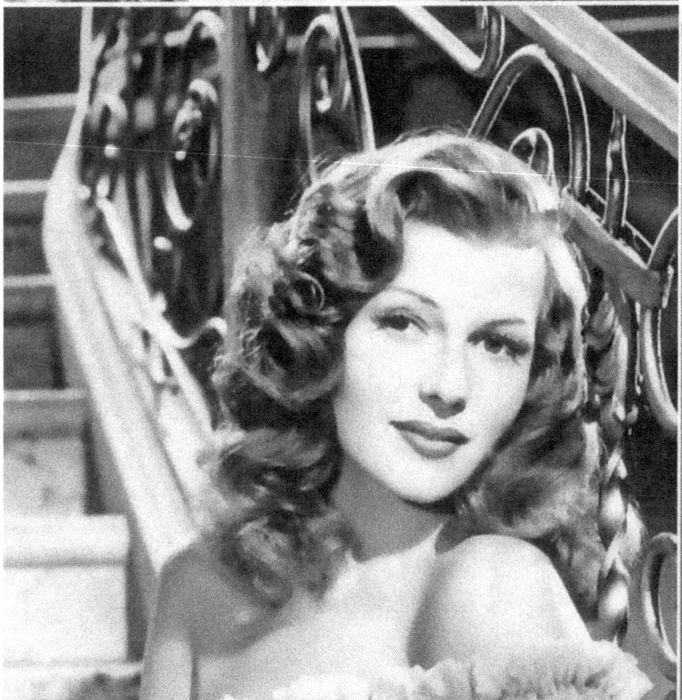
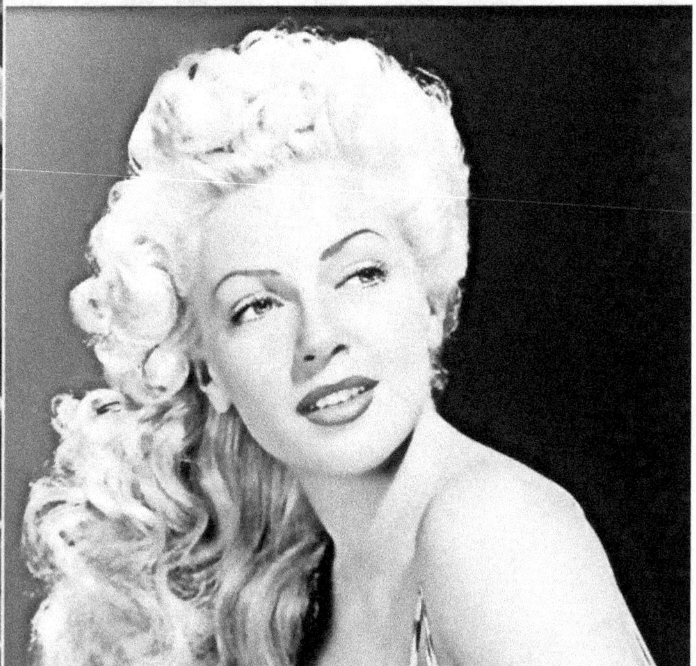

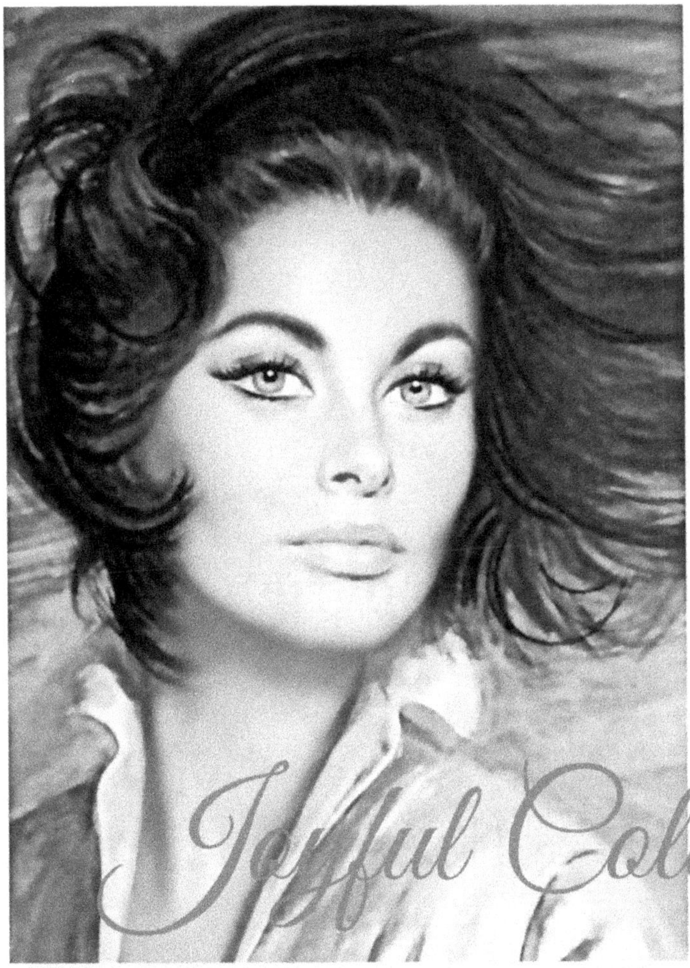

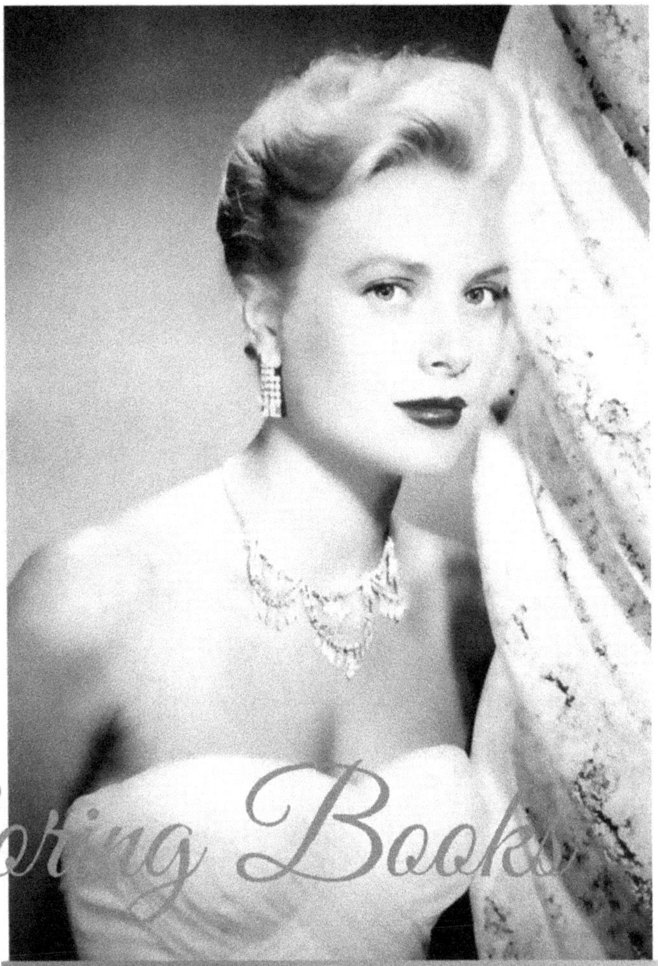

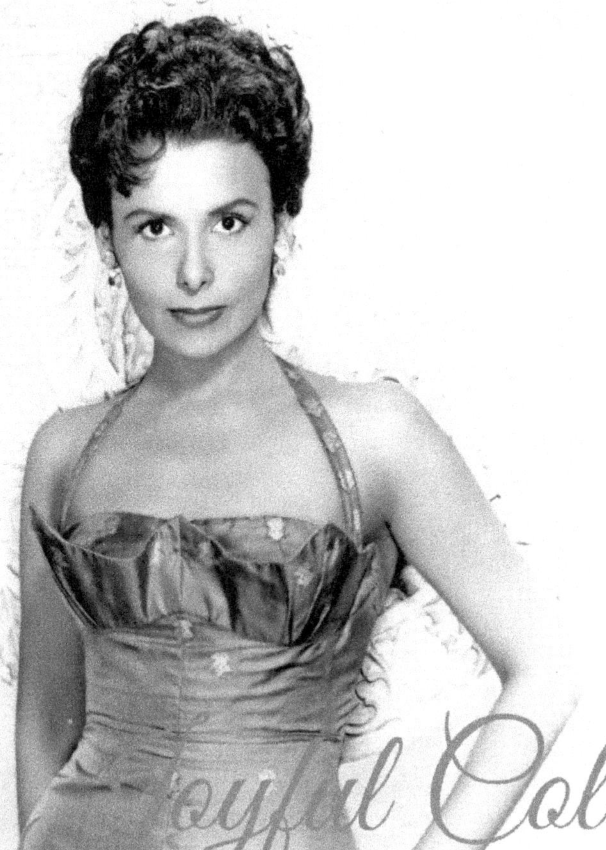

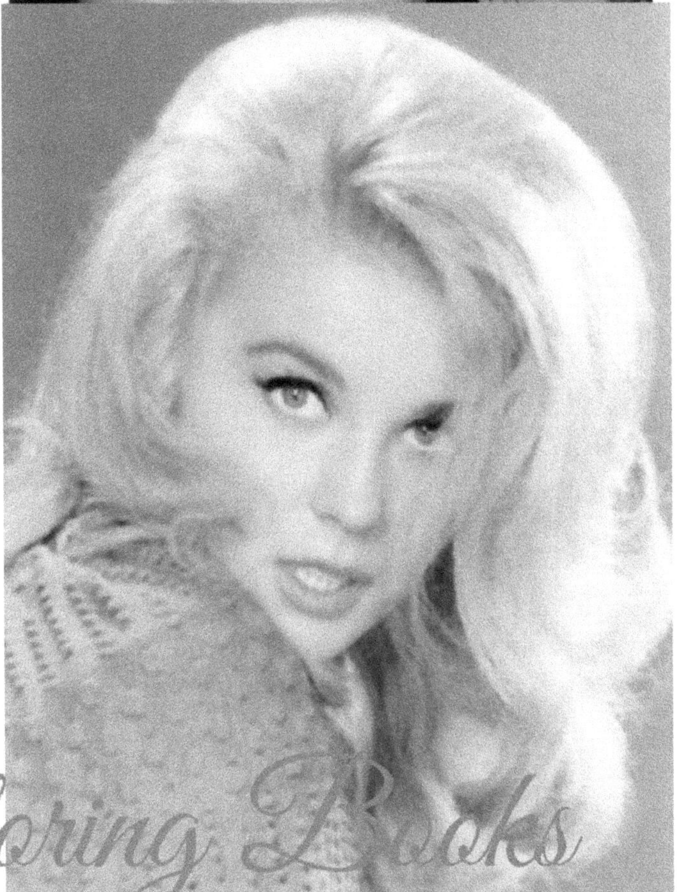

Copyright

ISBN-
10: 1-949152-24-3

ISBN-
13: 978-1-949152-24-1

Classic Pin-Ups

1-2. Elizabeth Taylor

3-4. Sophia Loren

5-6. Marilyn Monroe

7-8. Audrey Hepburn

9.　Katharine Hepburn

10.　Grace Kelly

11.　Vivian Leigh

12.　Bette Davis

13.　Ginger Rogers

14.　Lana Turner

15.　Ava Gardner

16.　Rita Hayworth

17.　Betty Grable

18.　Greta Garbo

19.　Maureen O'Hara

20.　Gina Lollobrigida

21.　Lena Horne

22.　Judy Garland

23.　Lauren Bacall

24.　Ann-Margret

25.　Lauren Hutton

26.　Brigitte Bardot

27.　Ursula Andress

28.　Raquel Welch

29-30.　Mae West

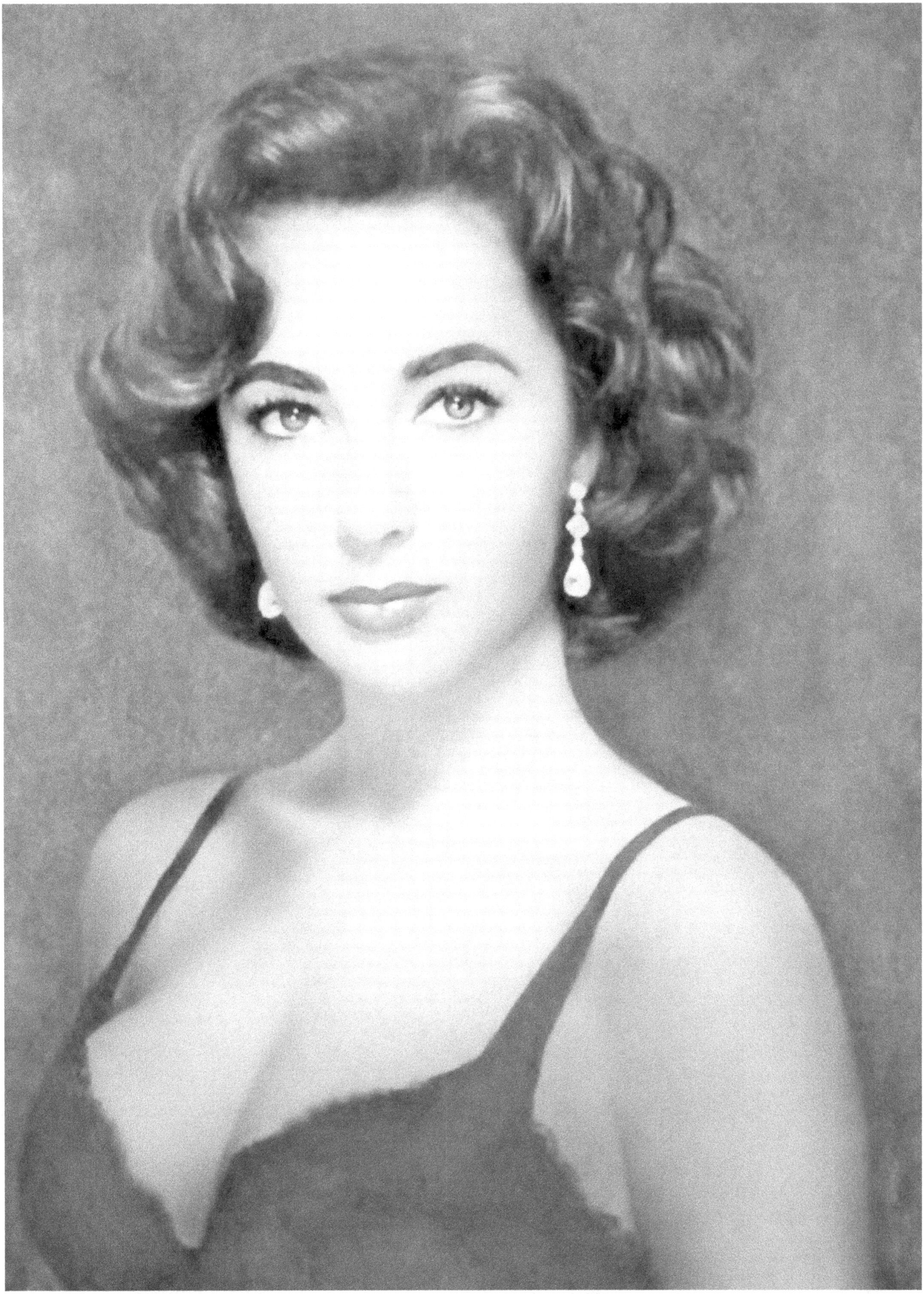

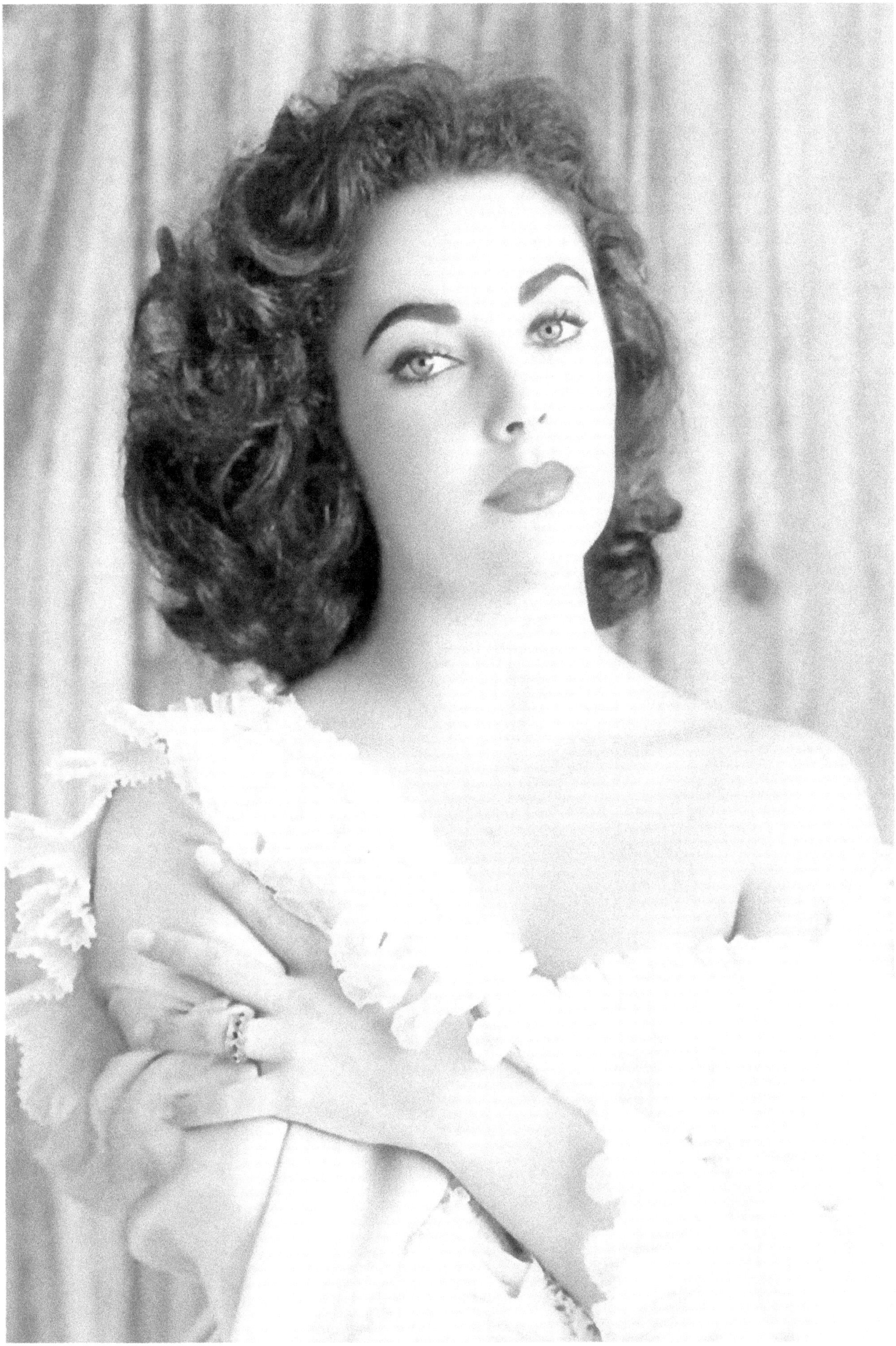

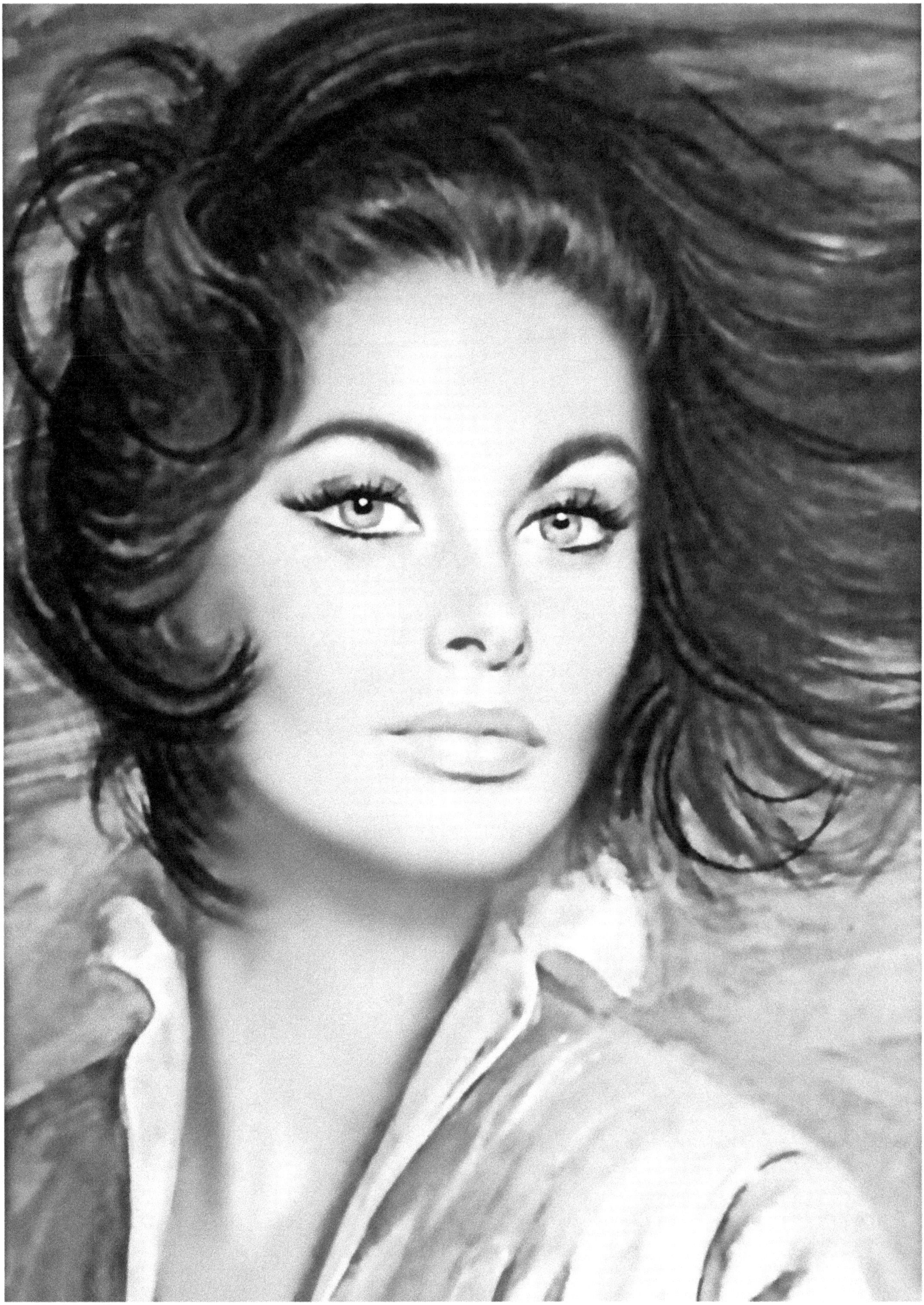

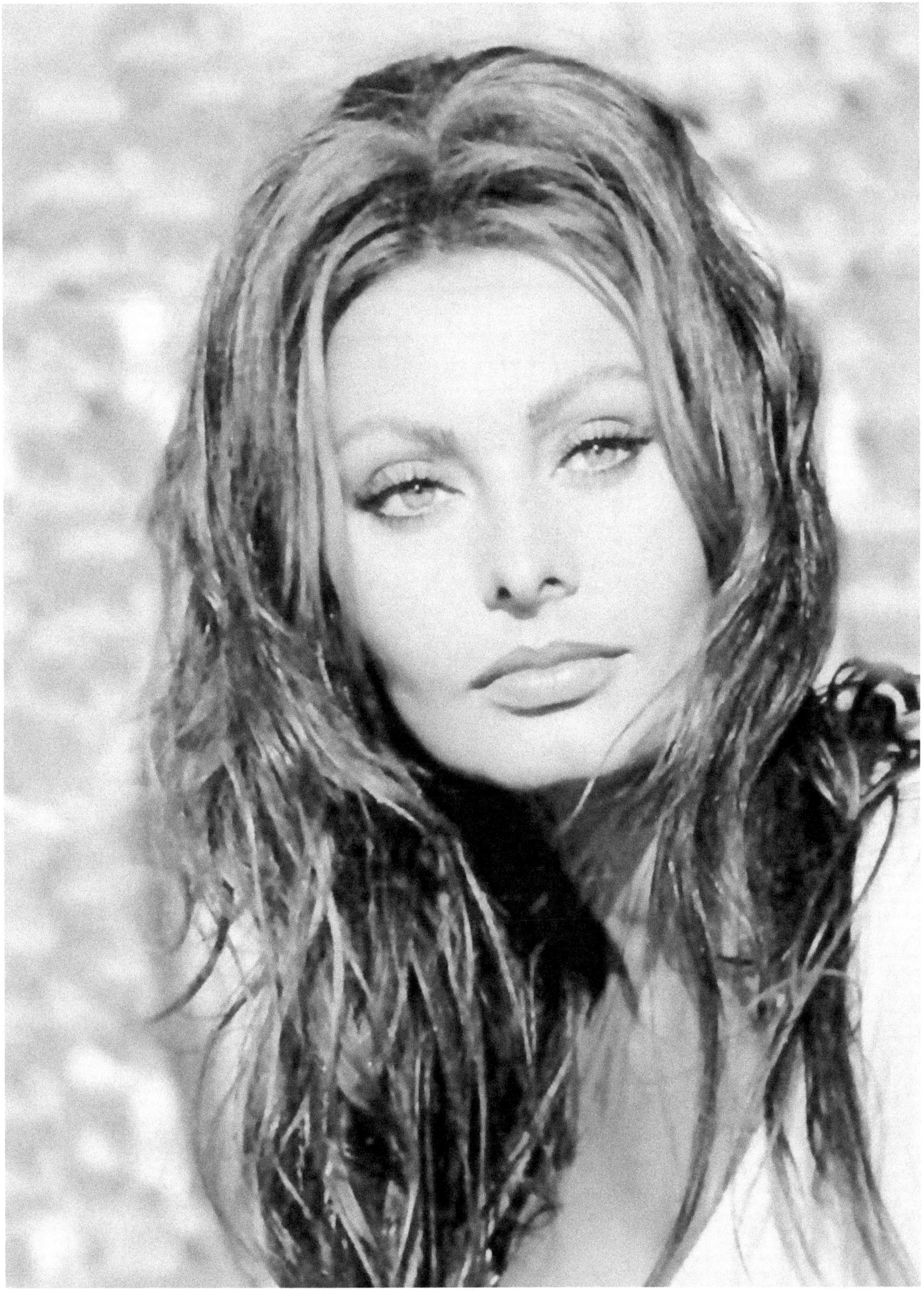

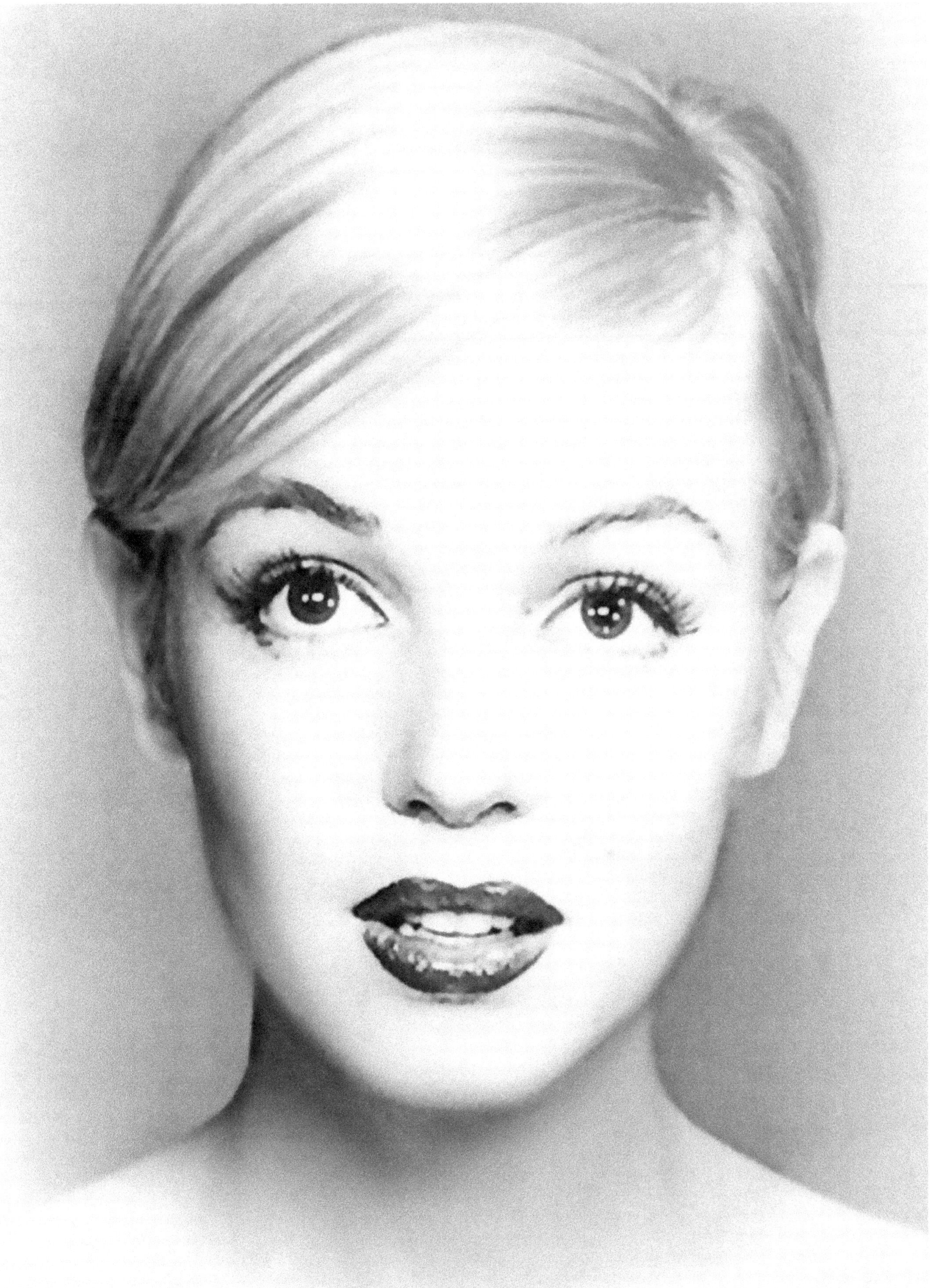

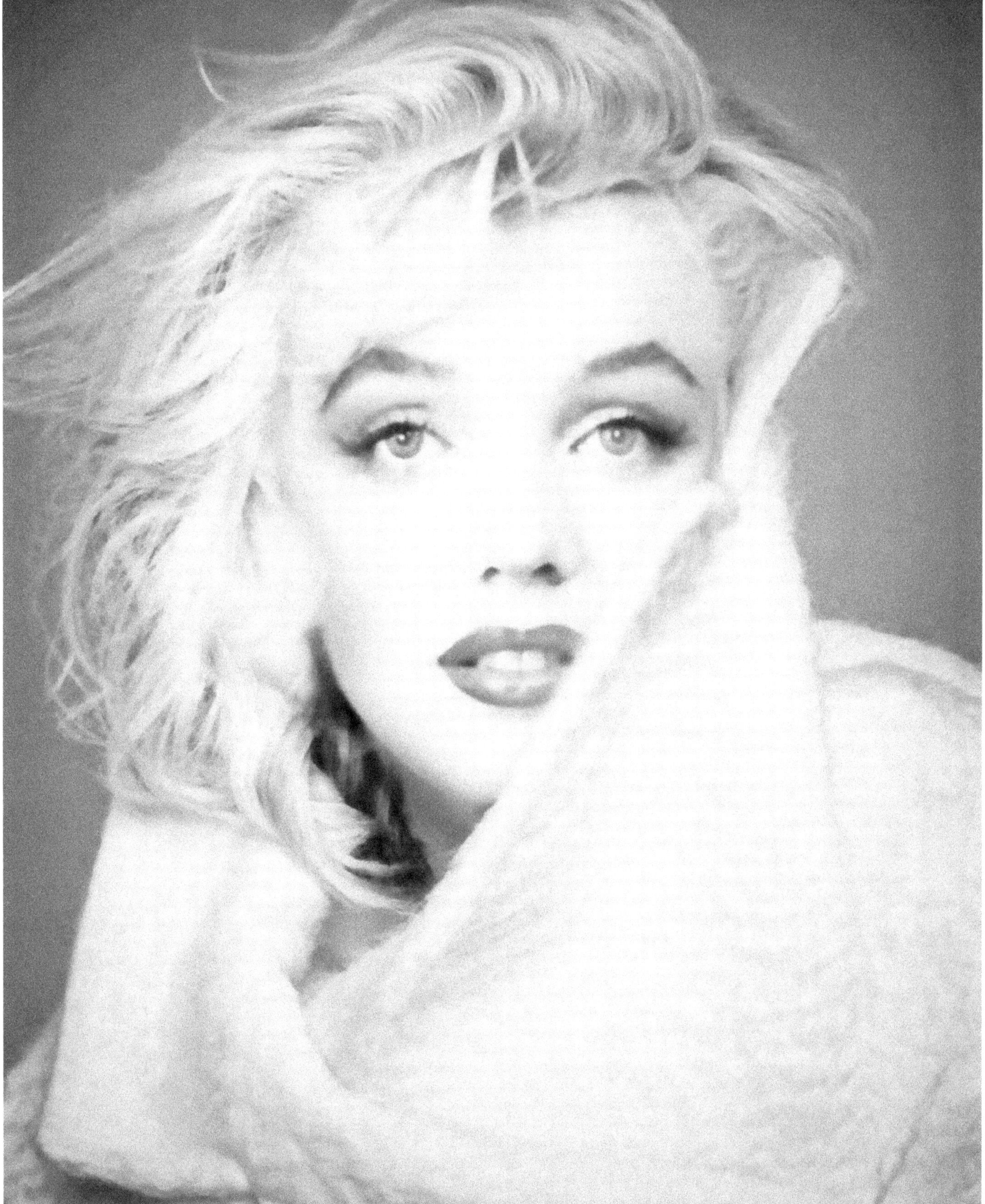

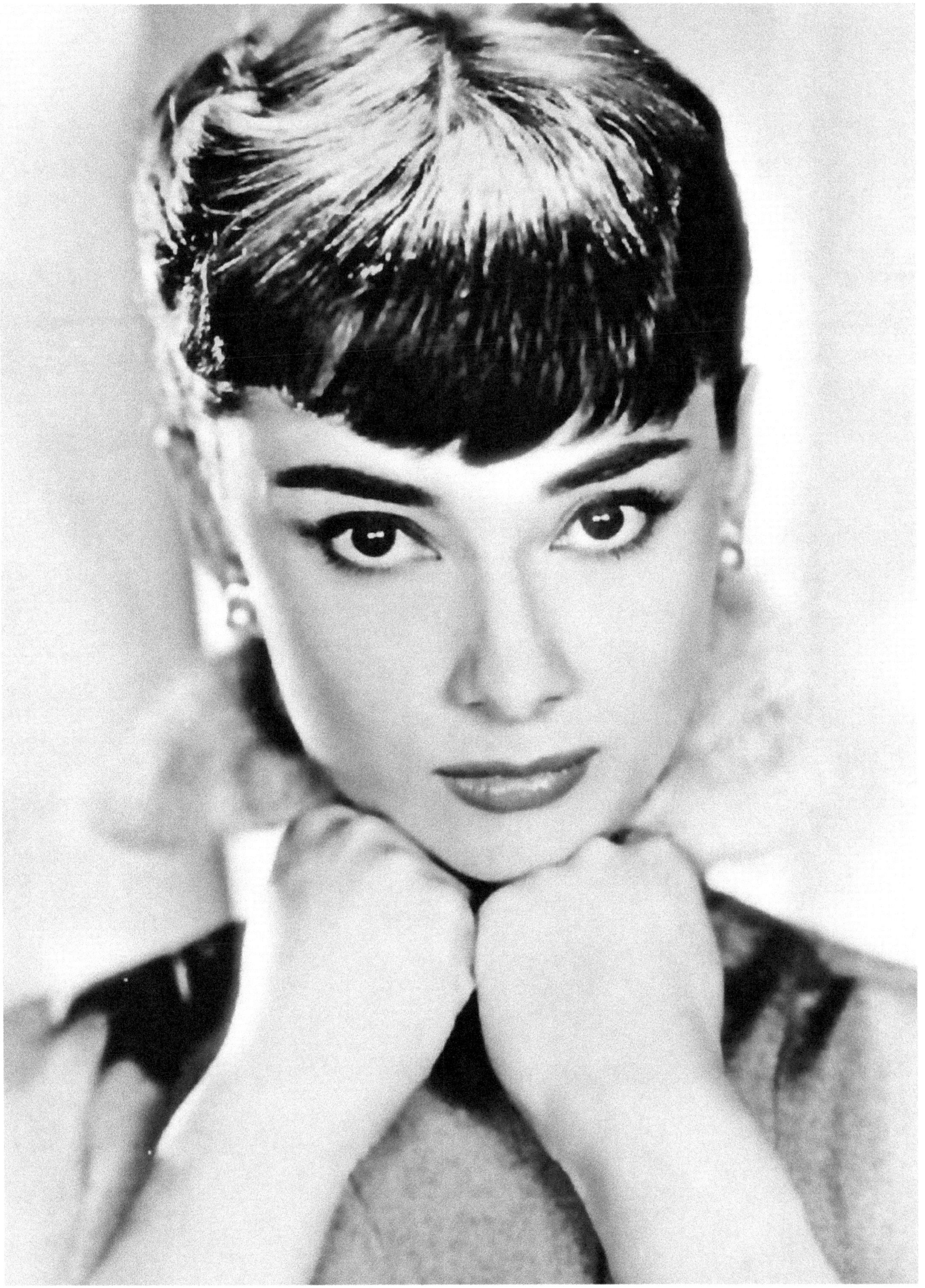

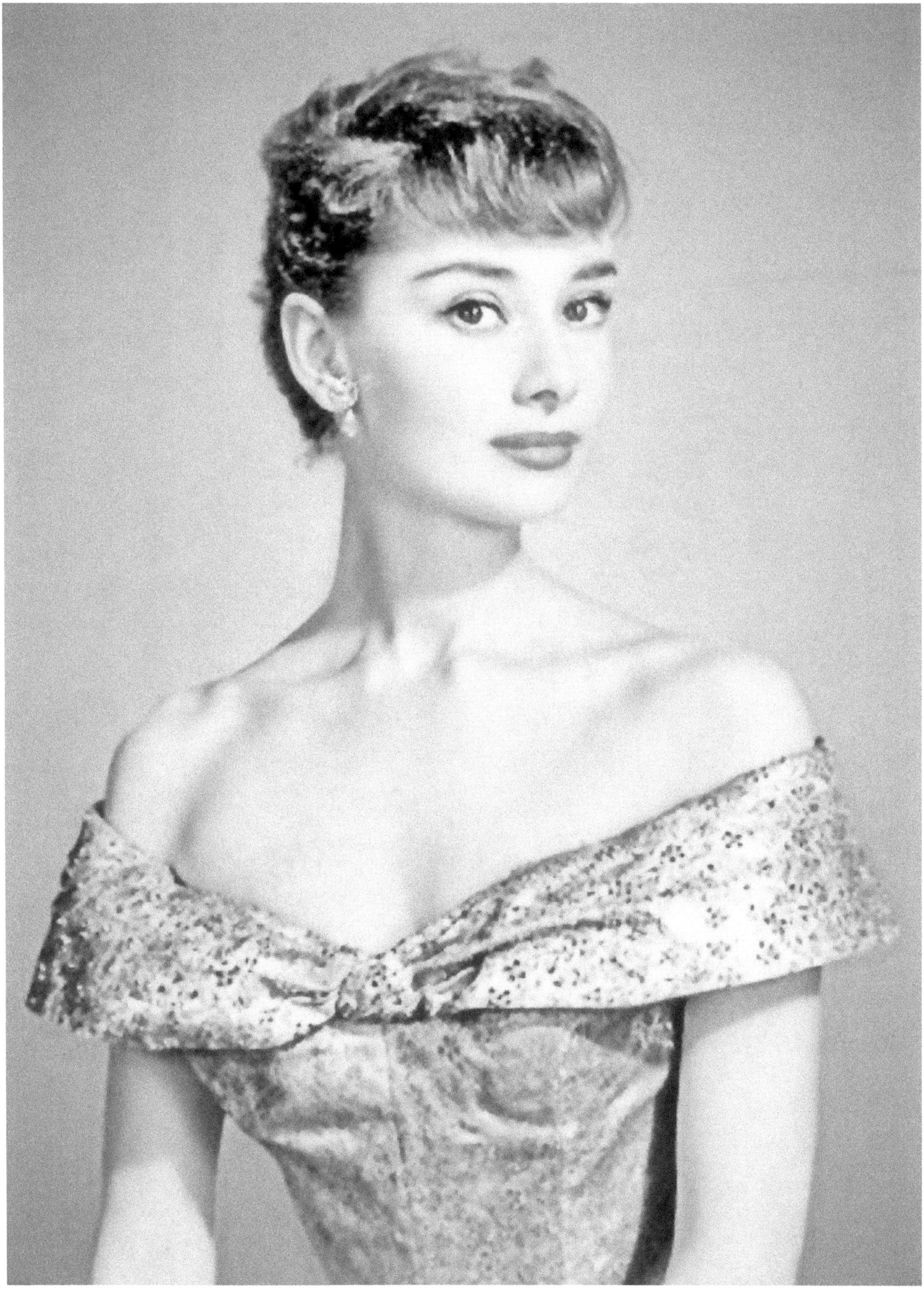

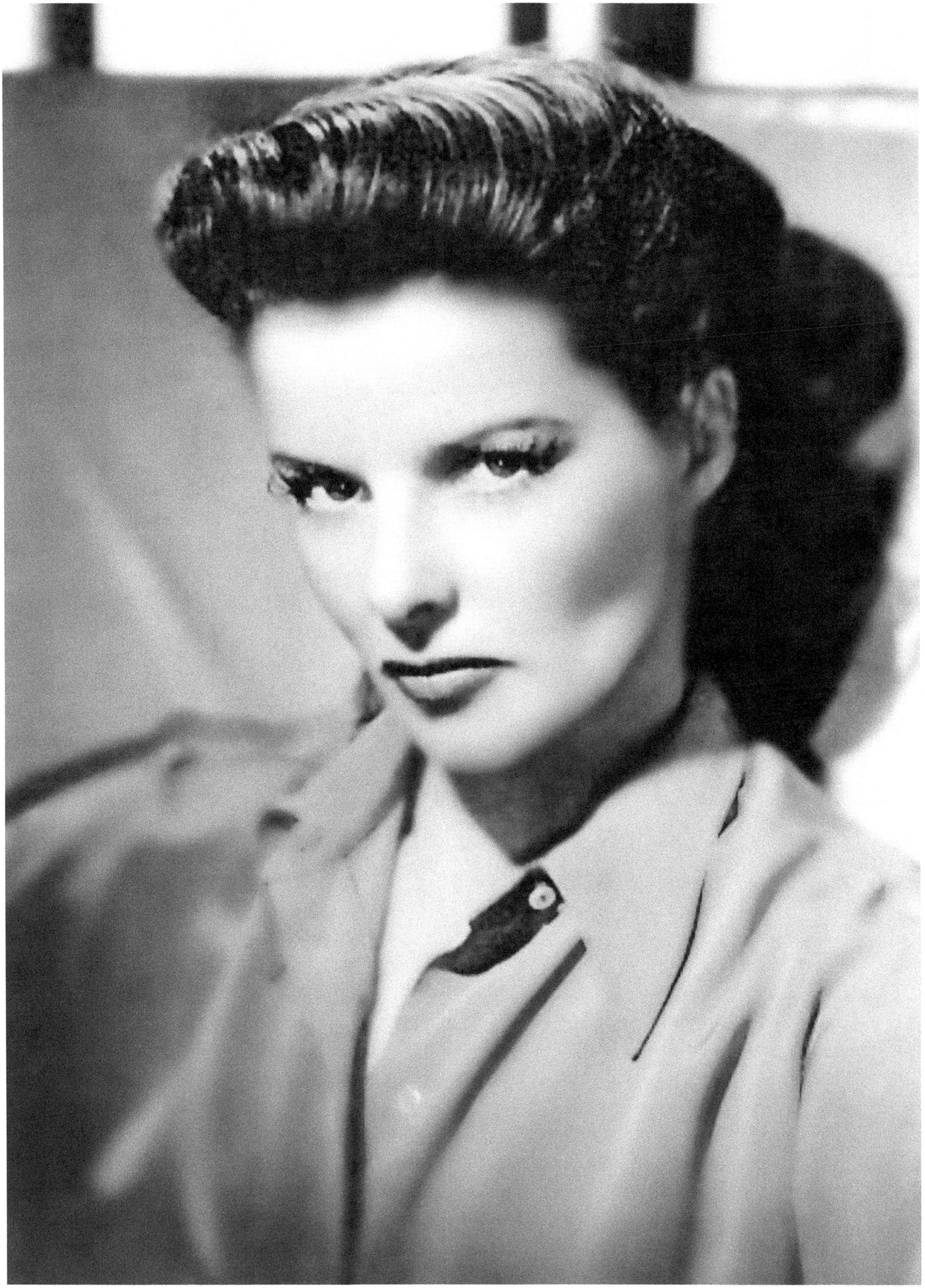

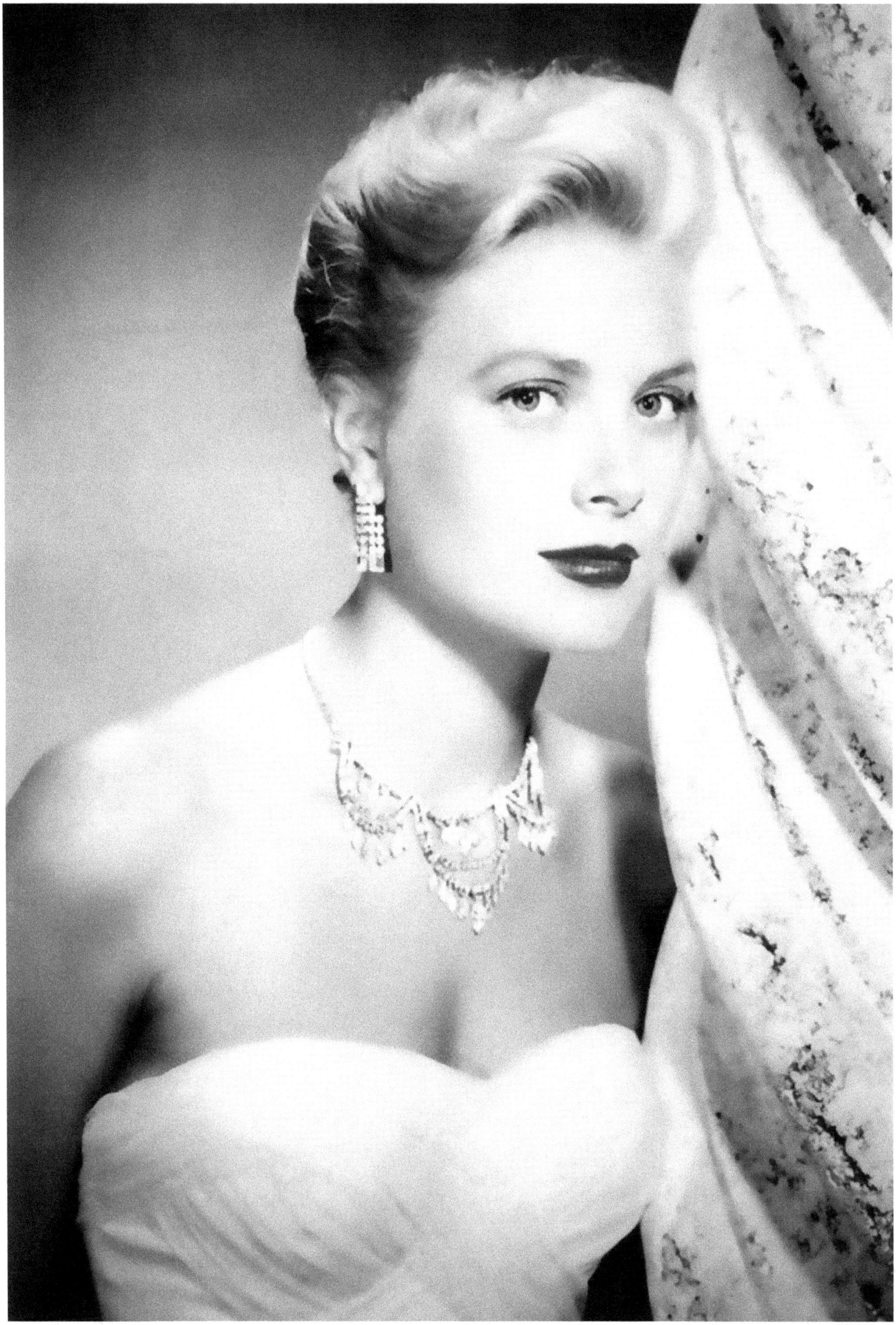

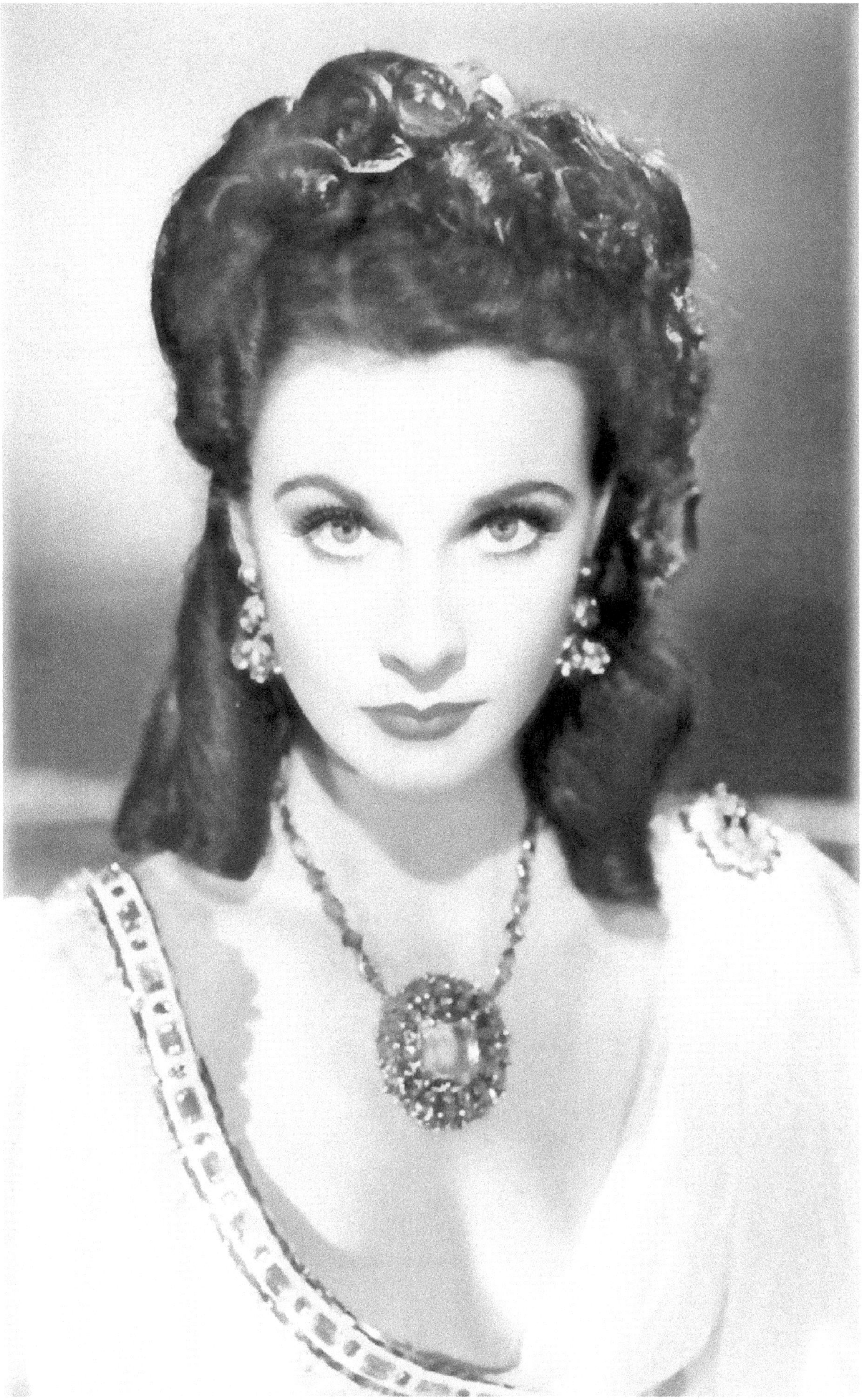

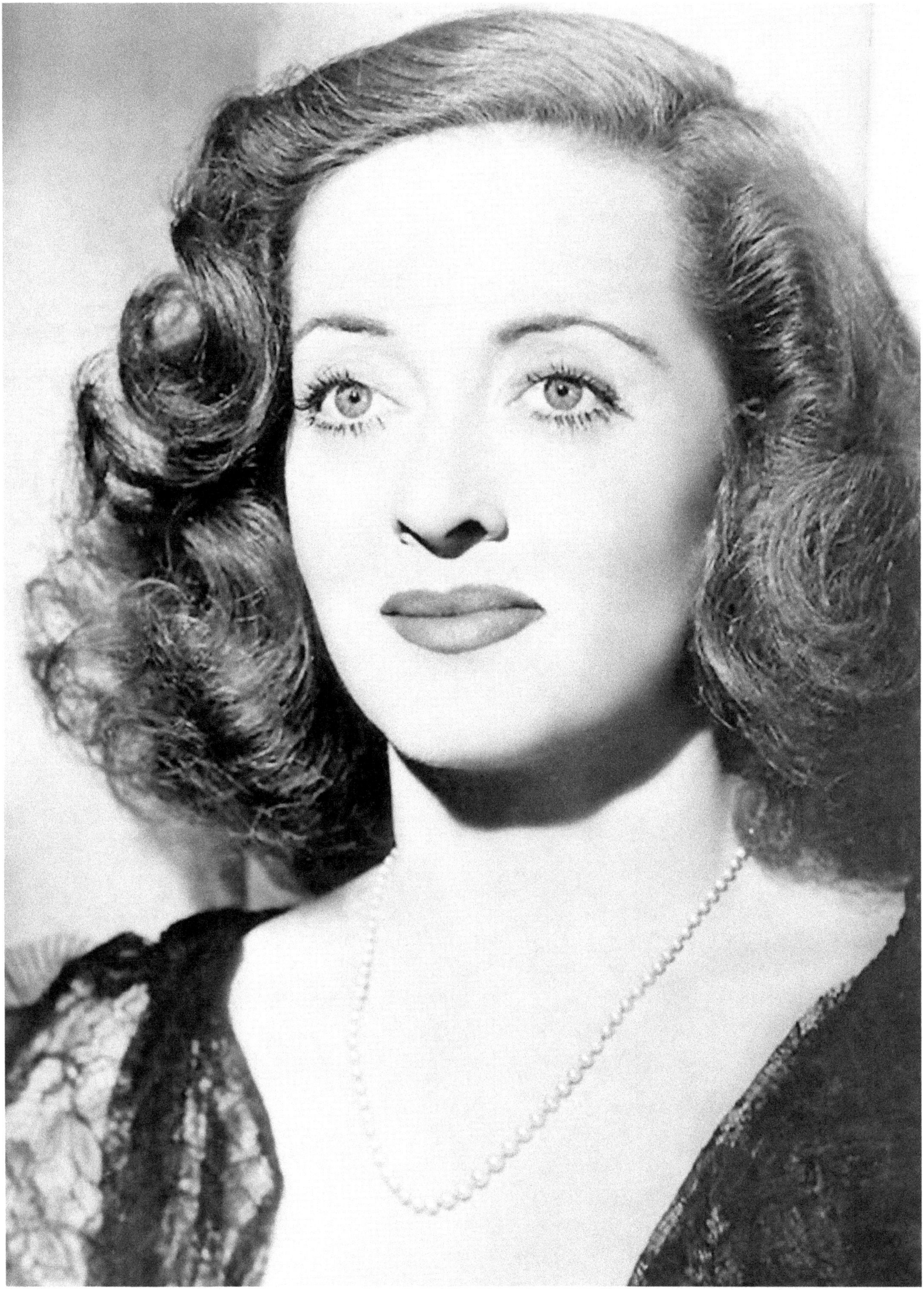

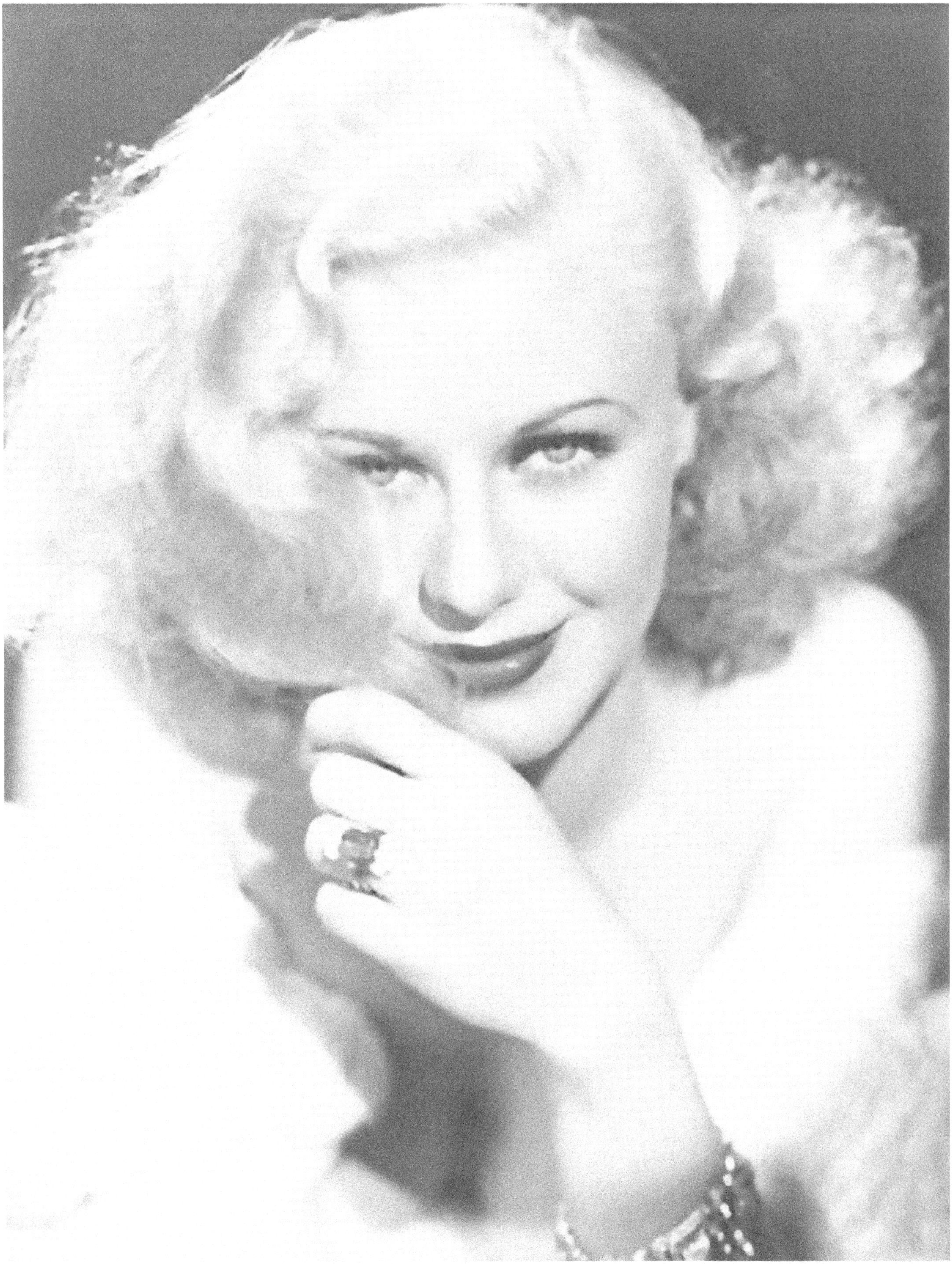

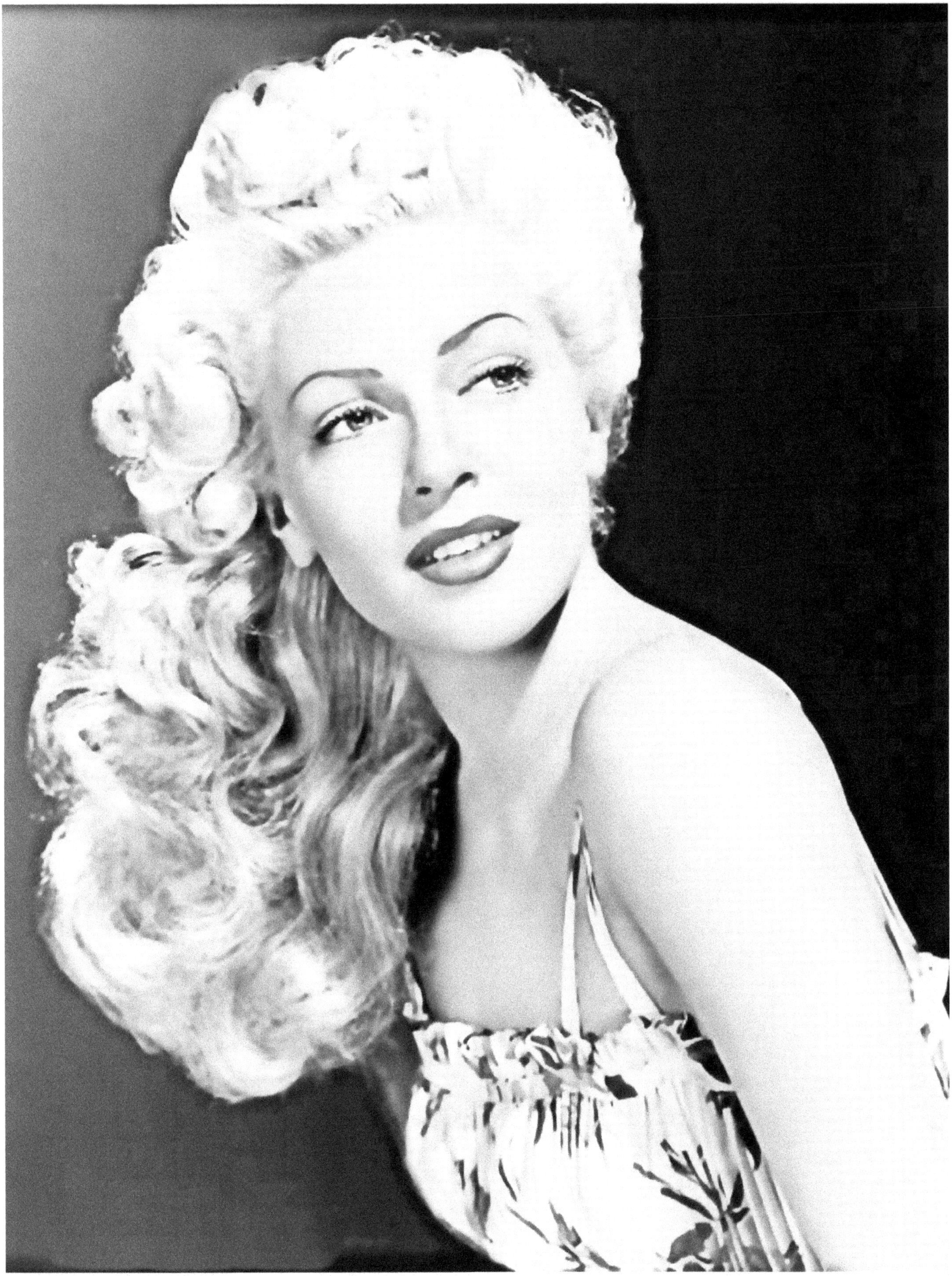

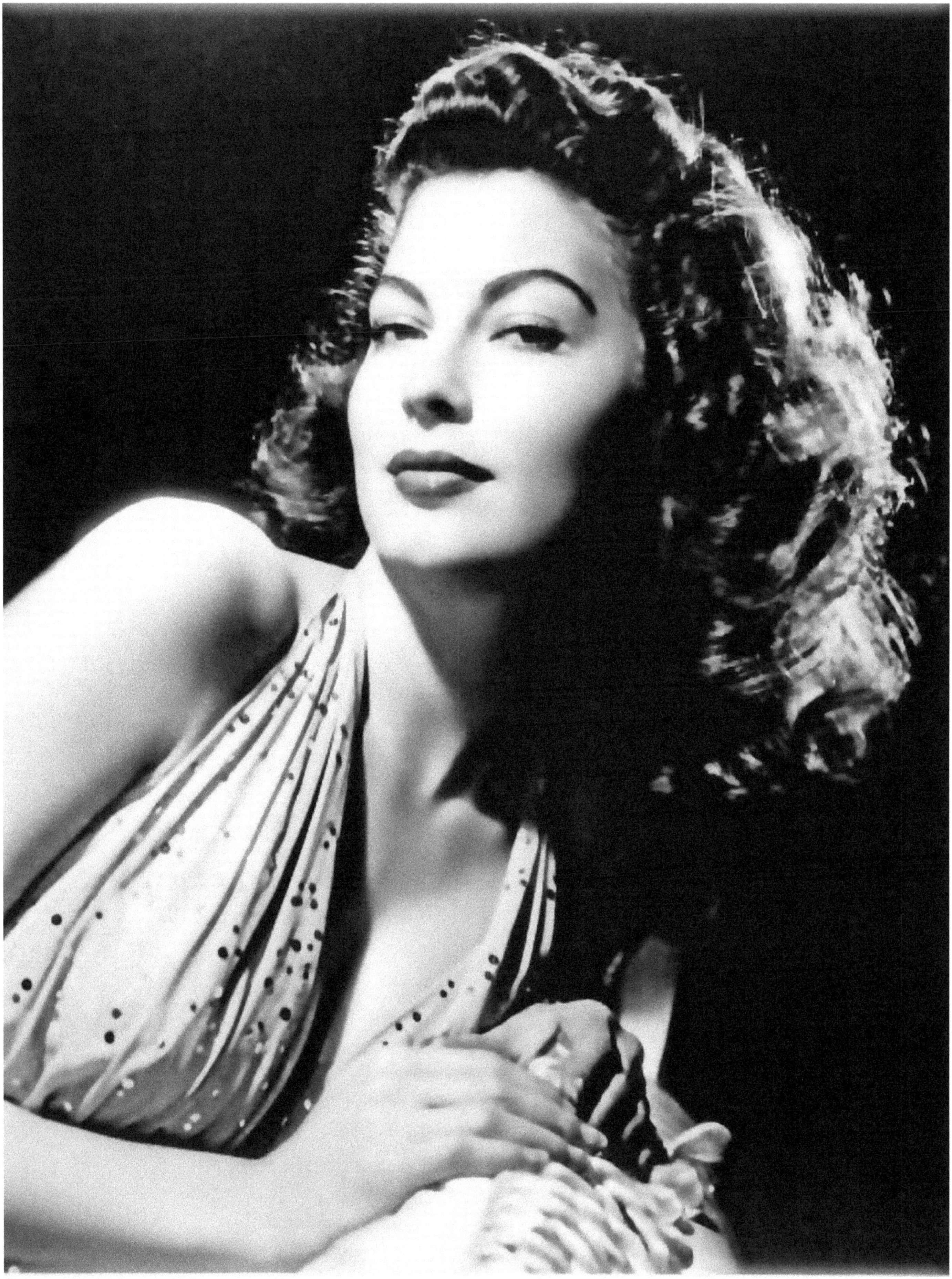

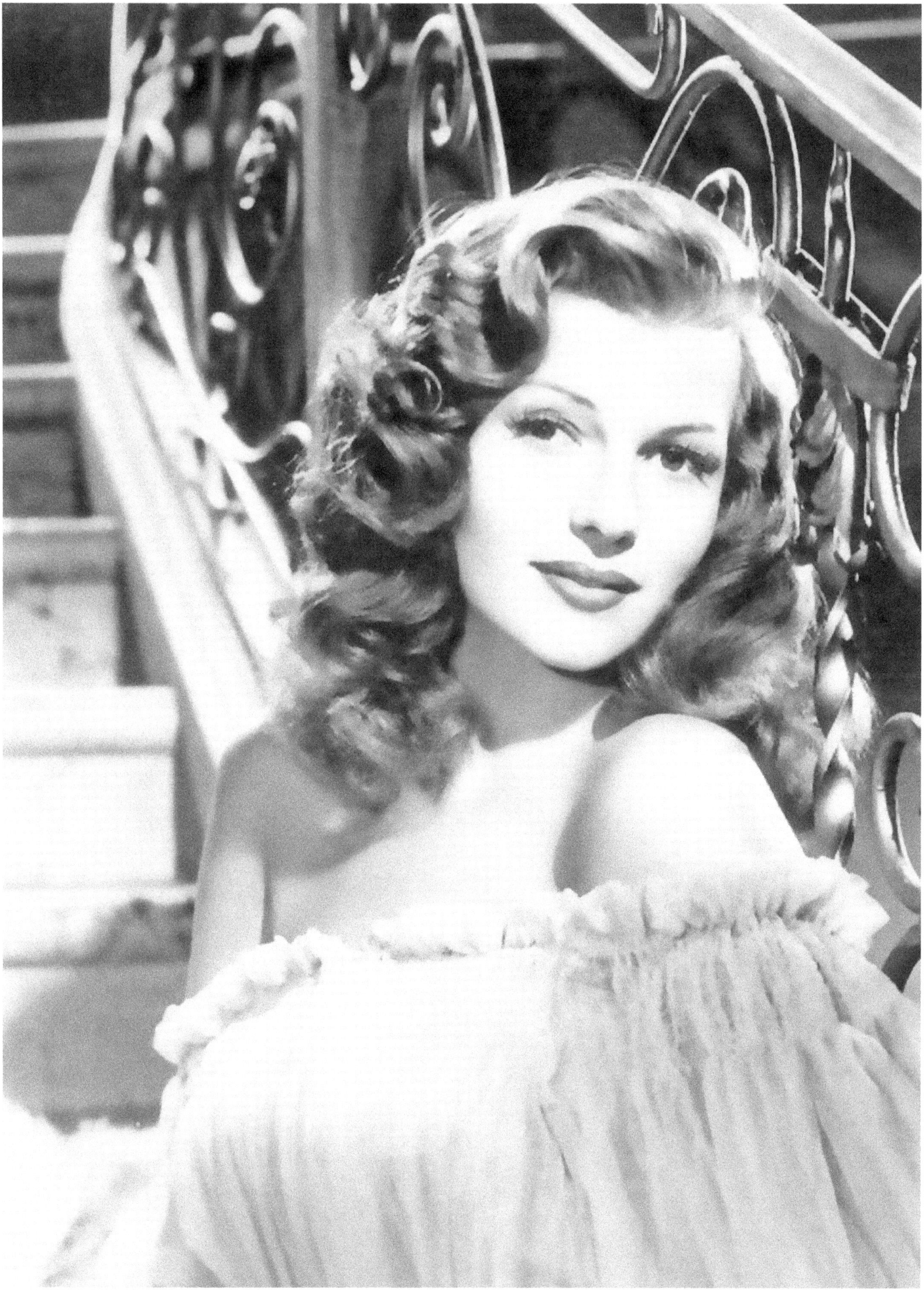

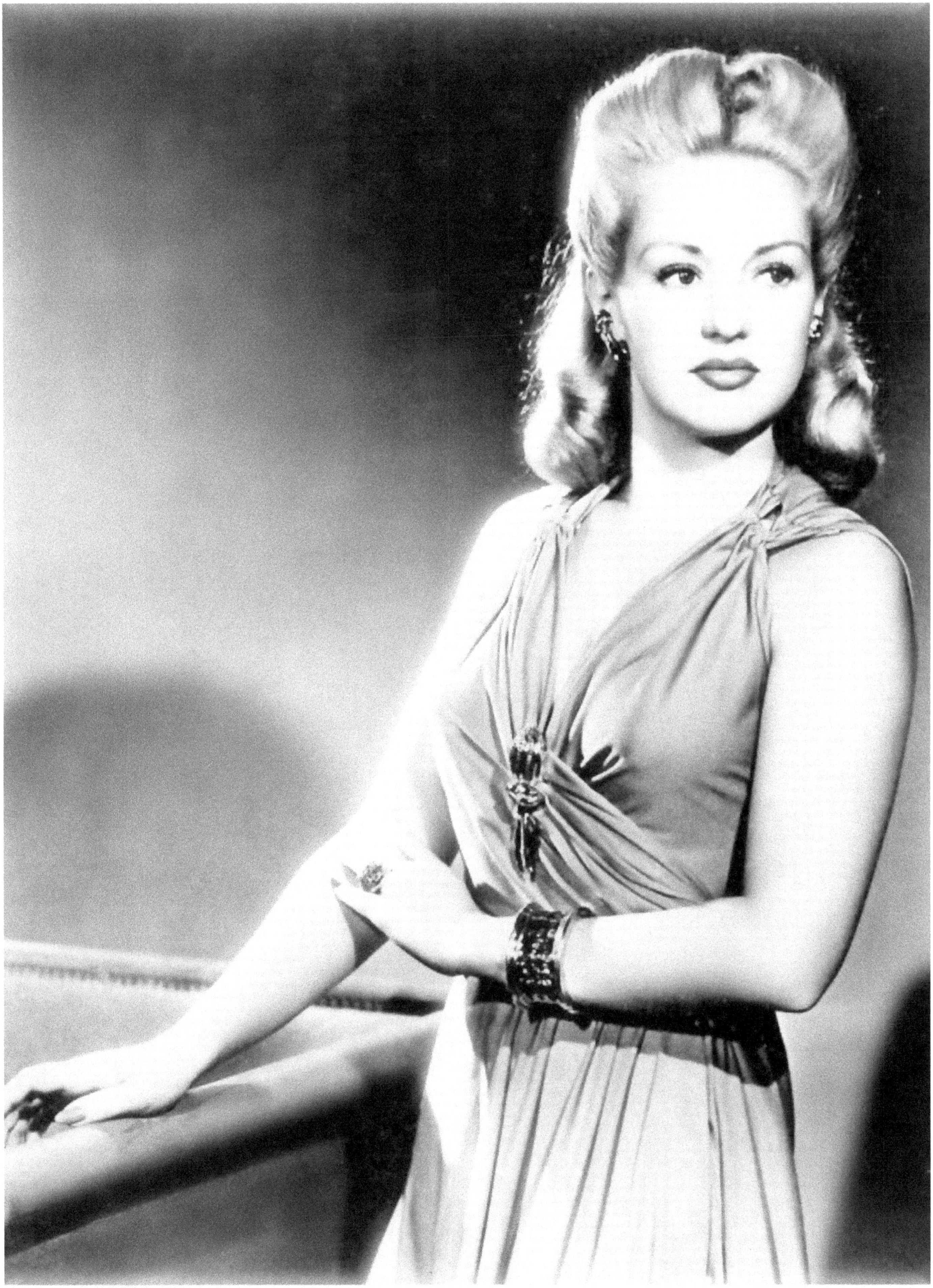

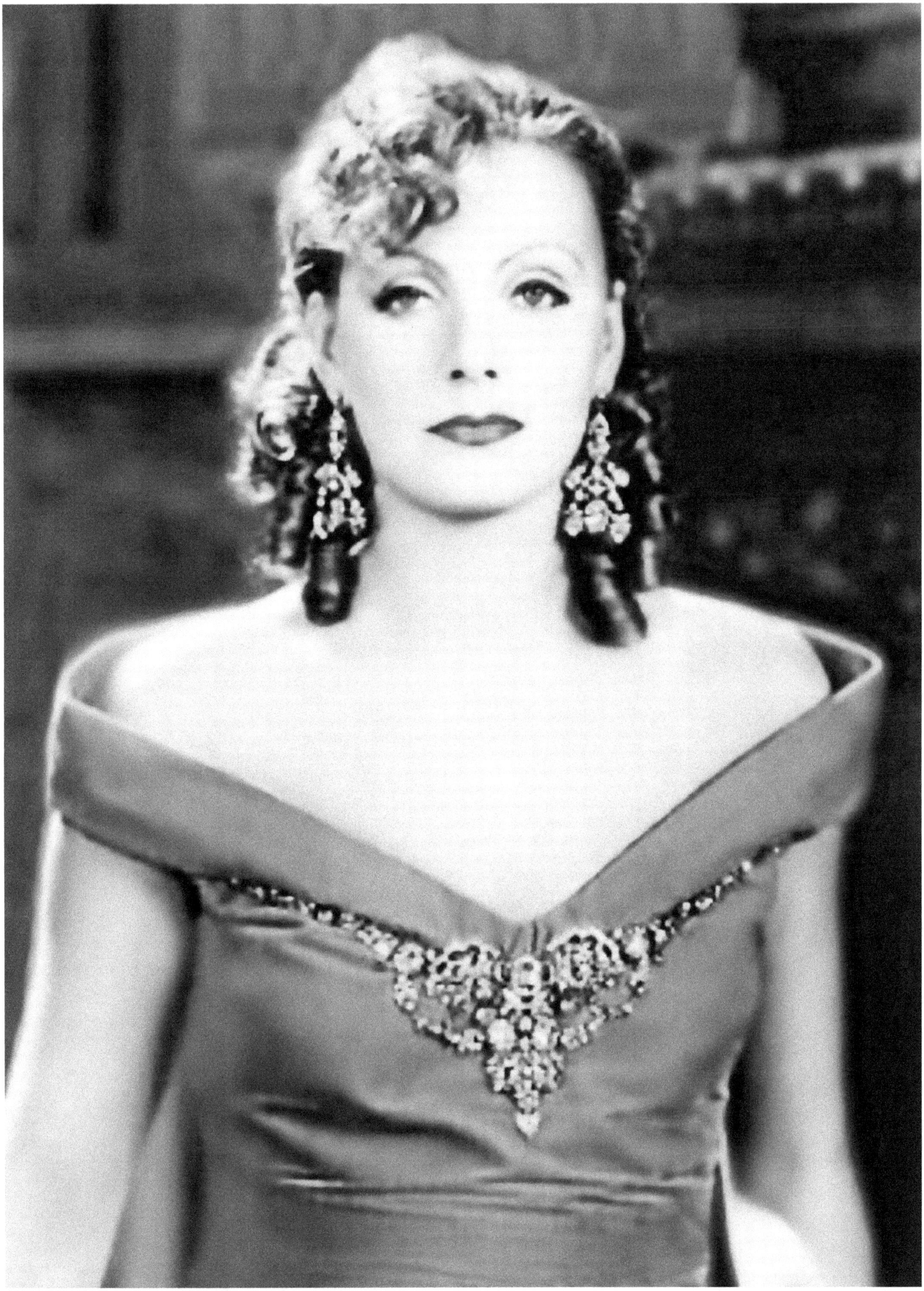

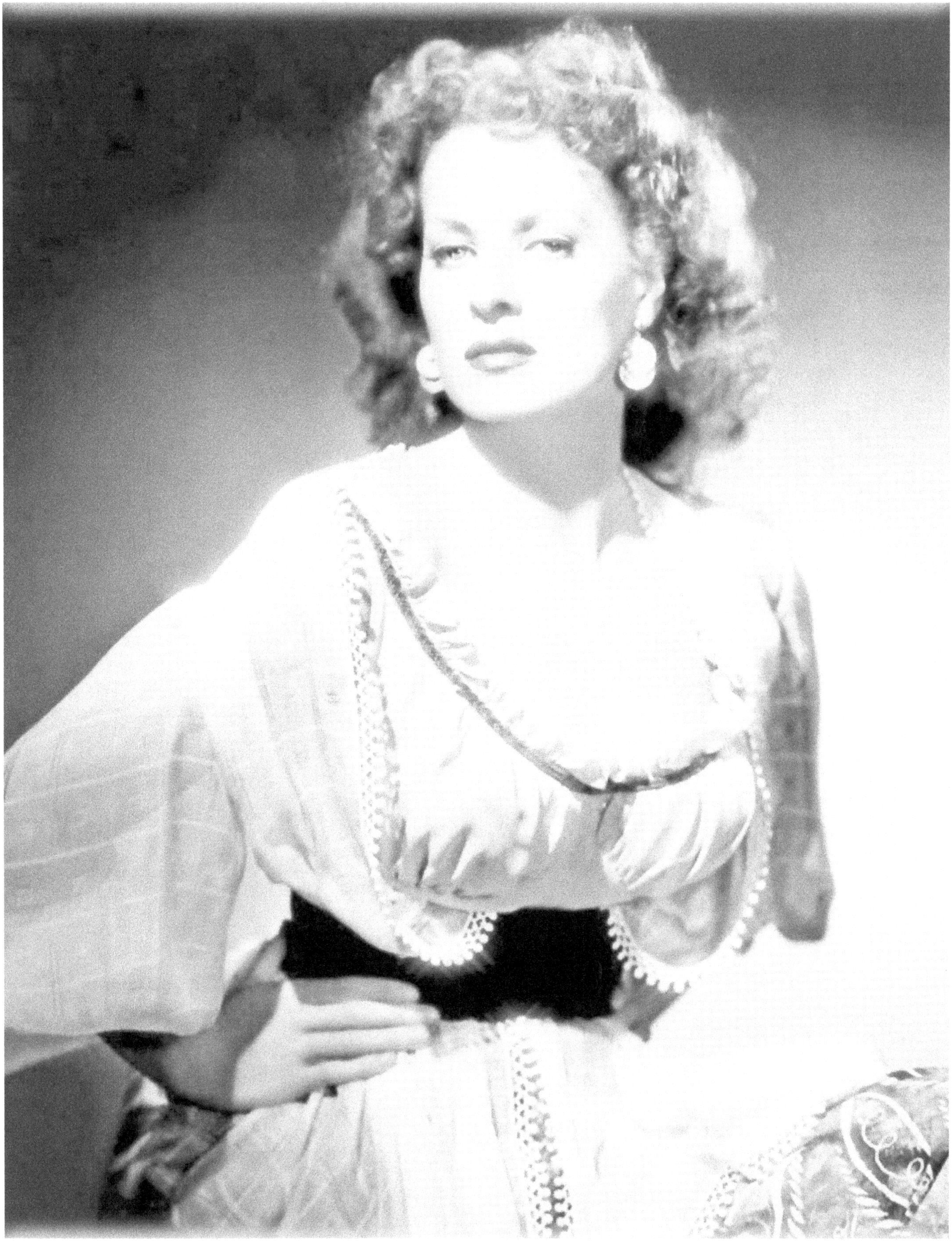

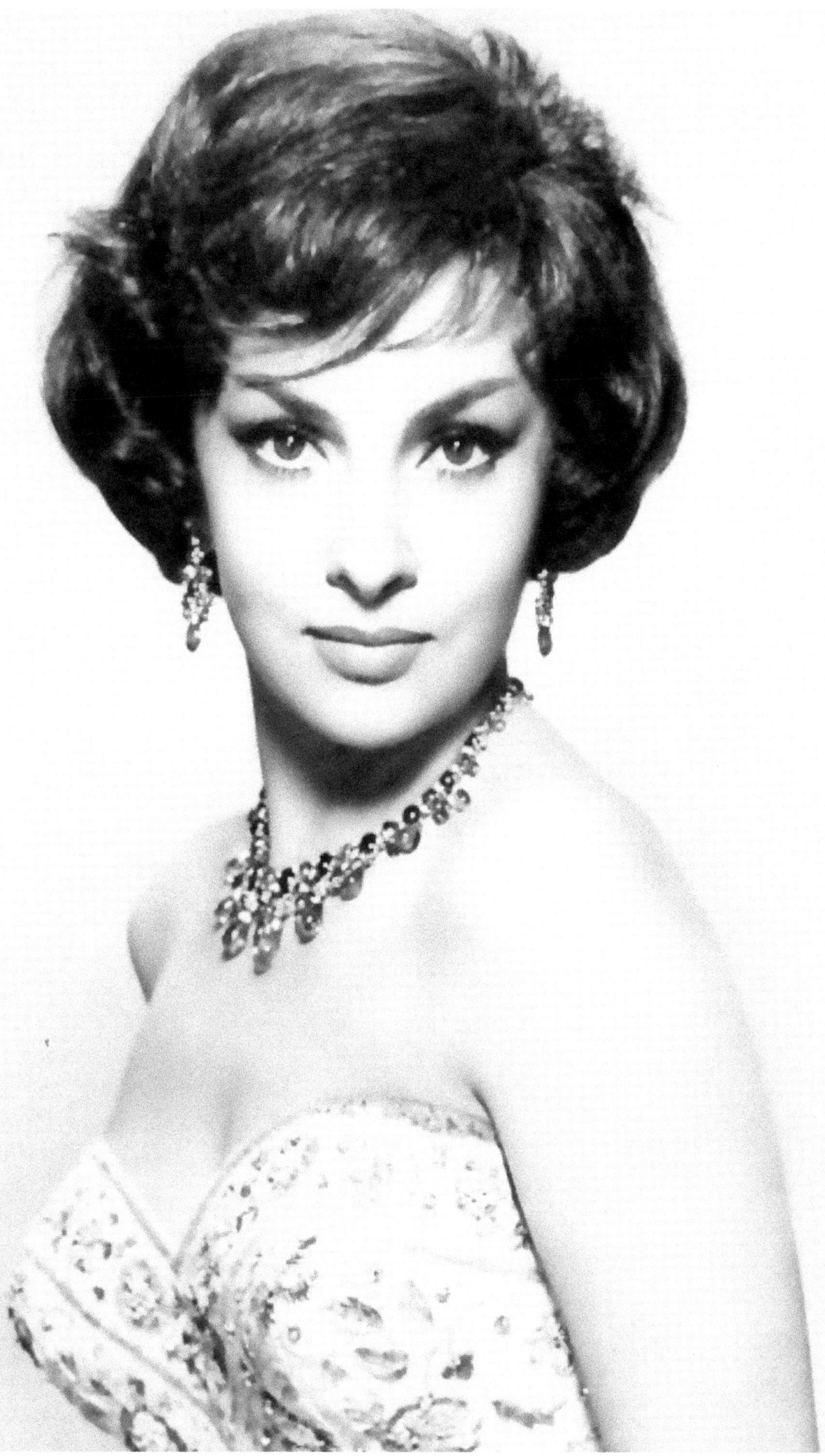

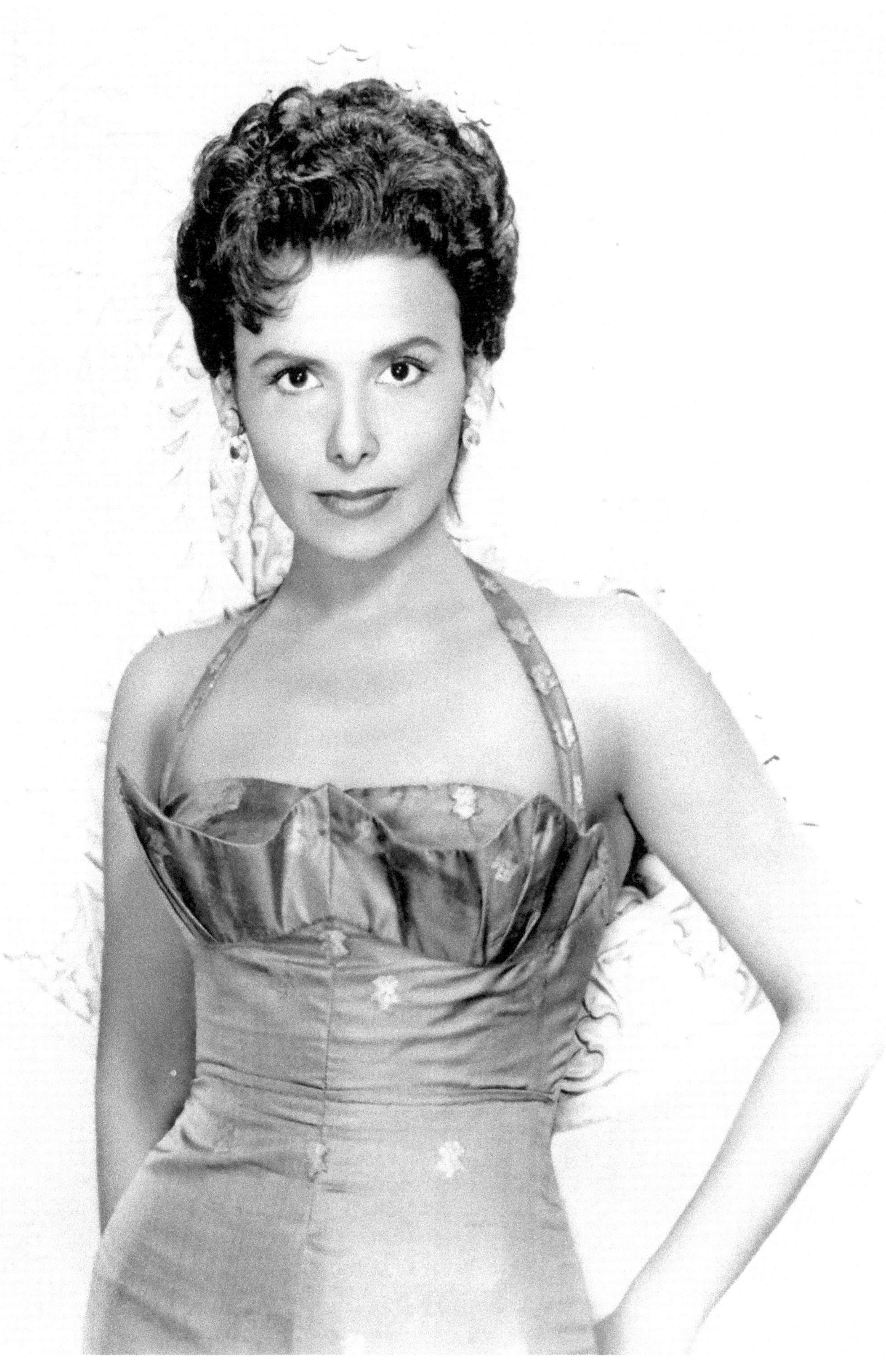

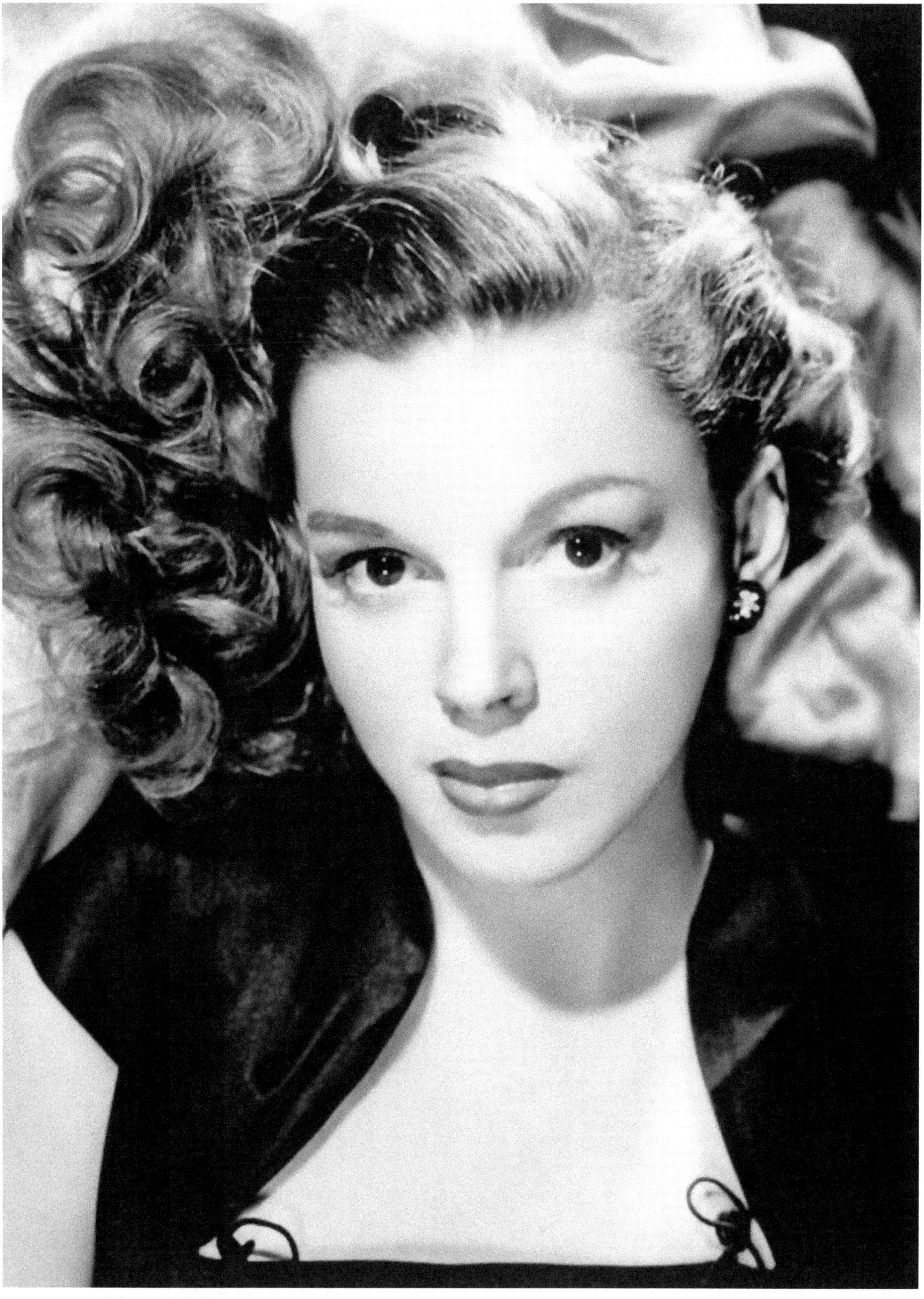

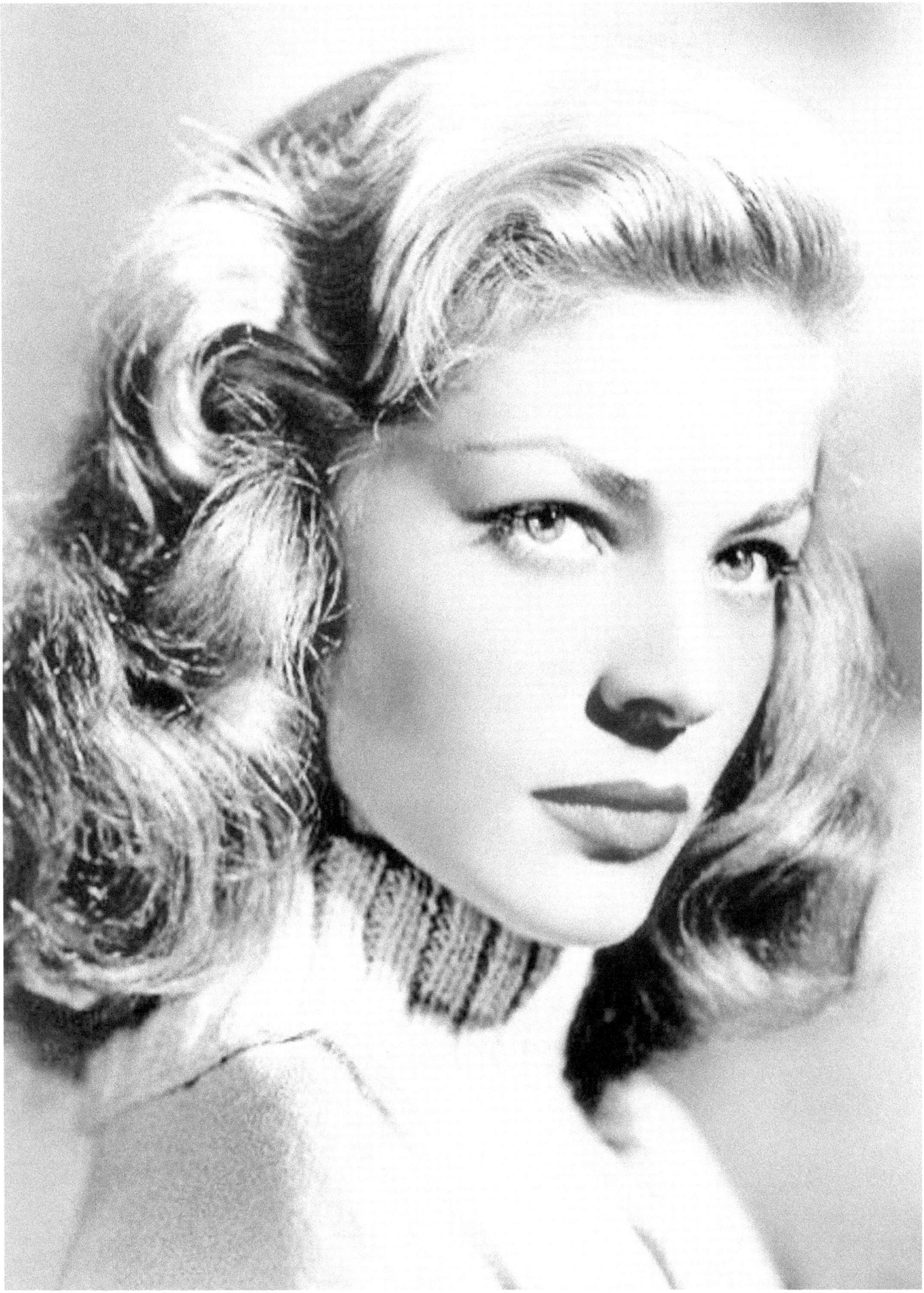

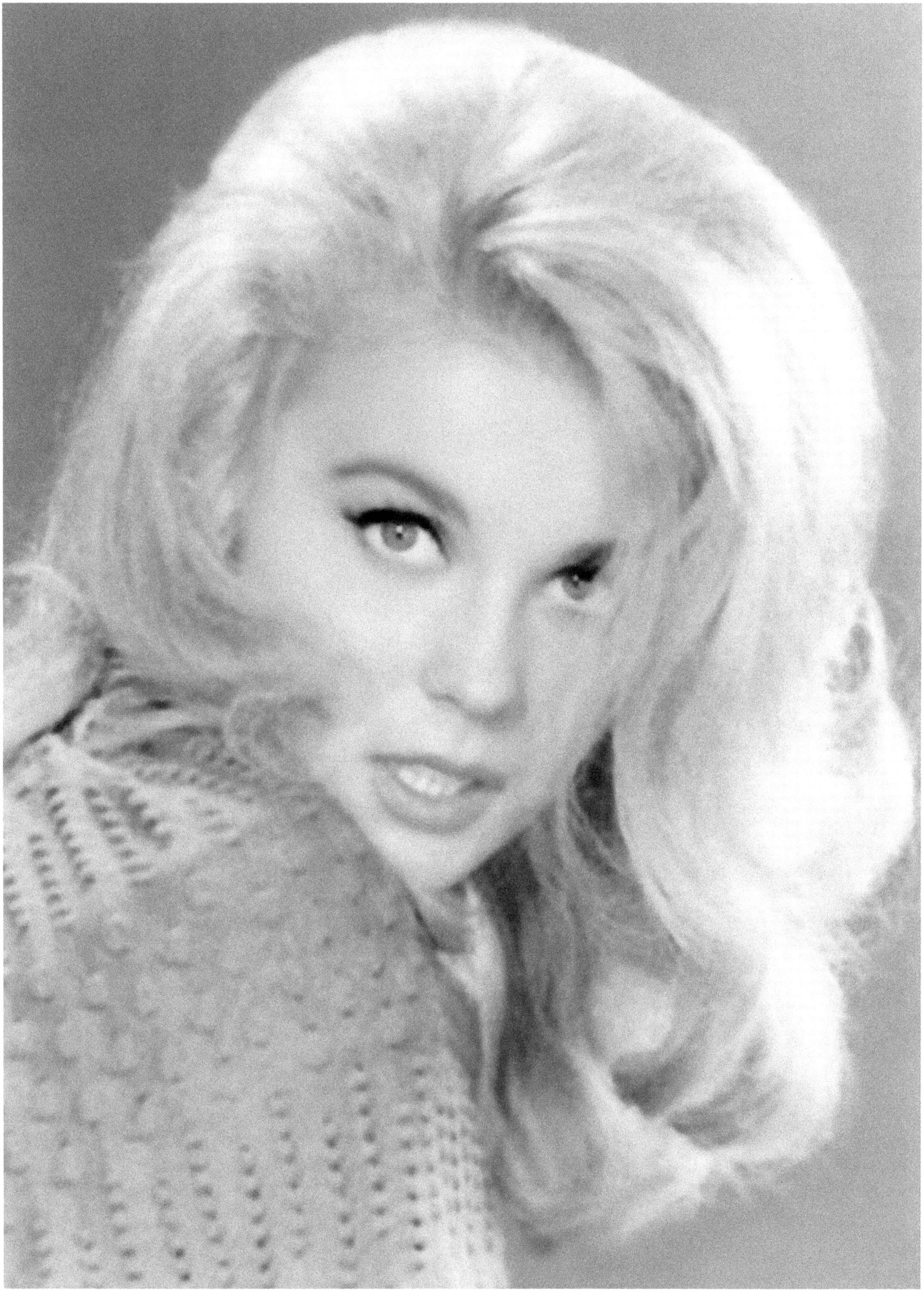

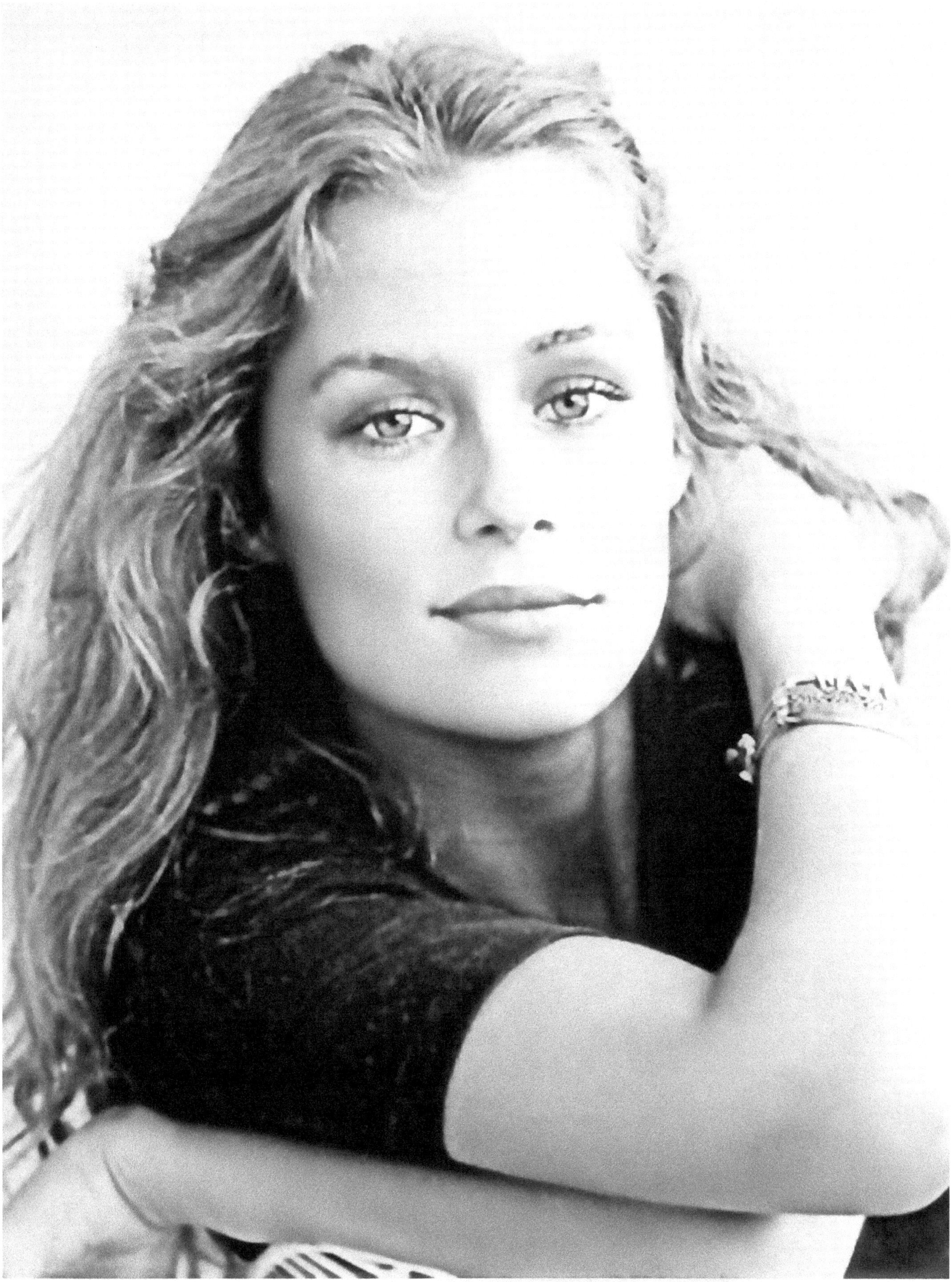

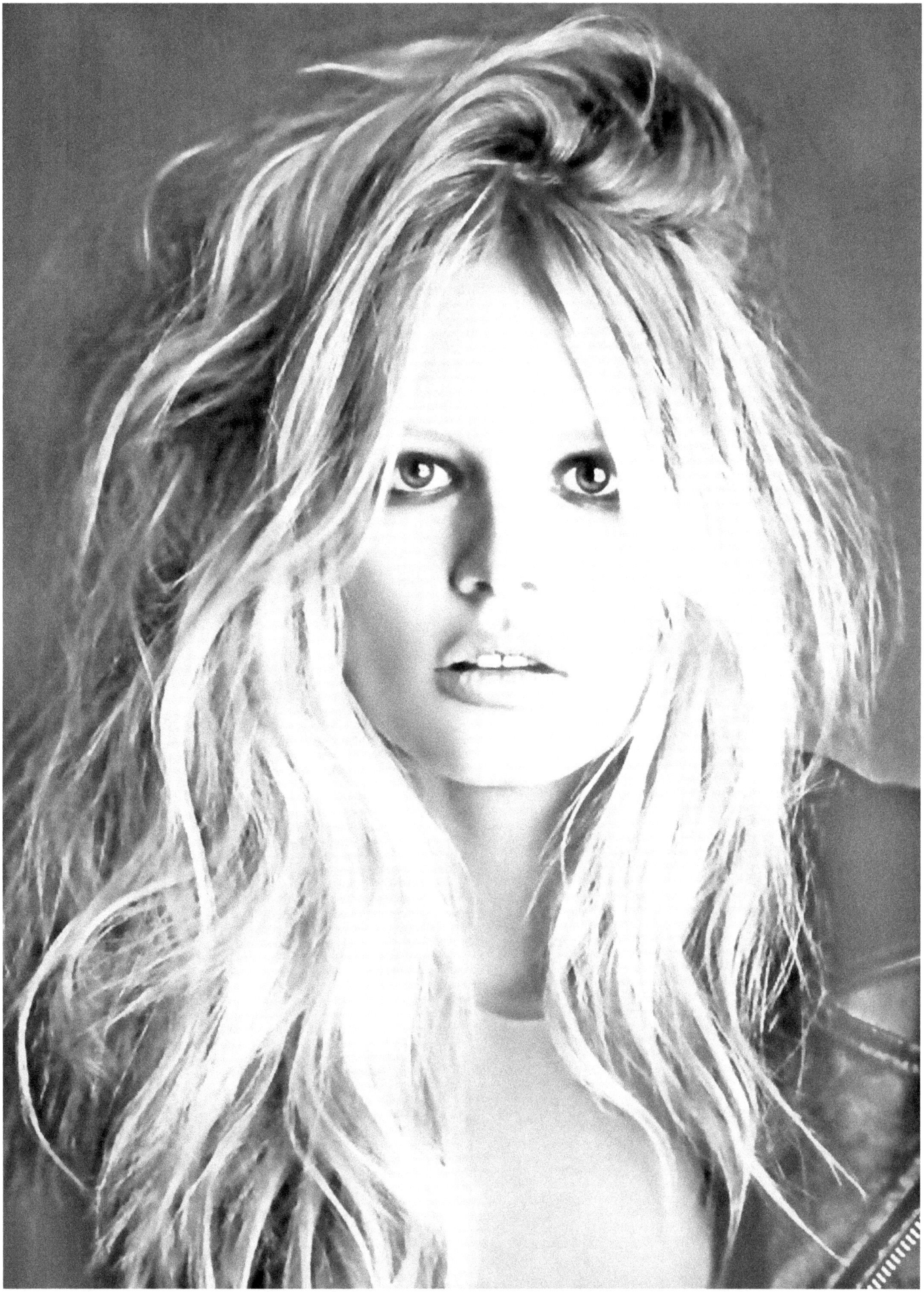

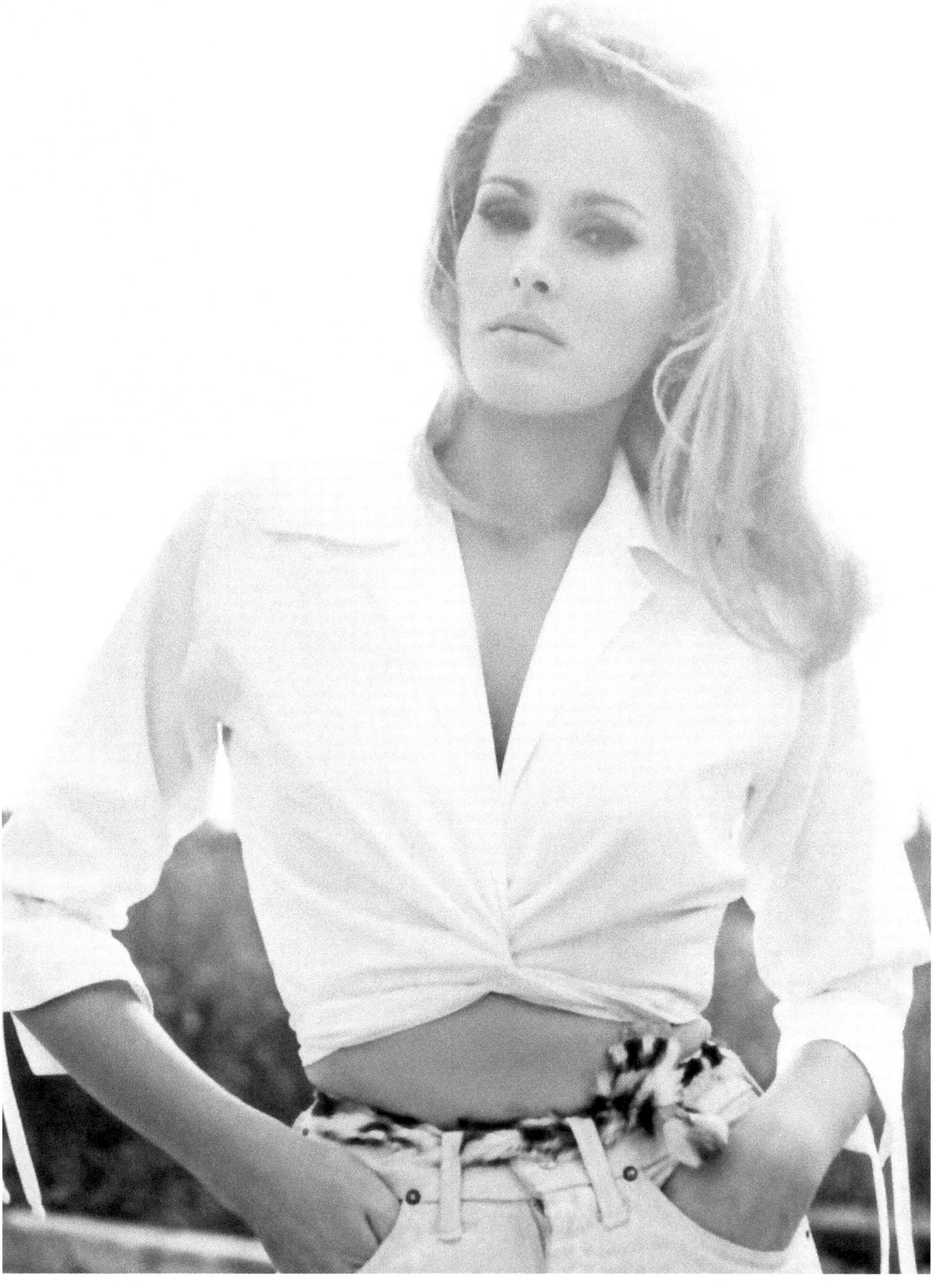

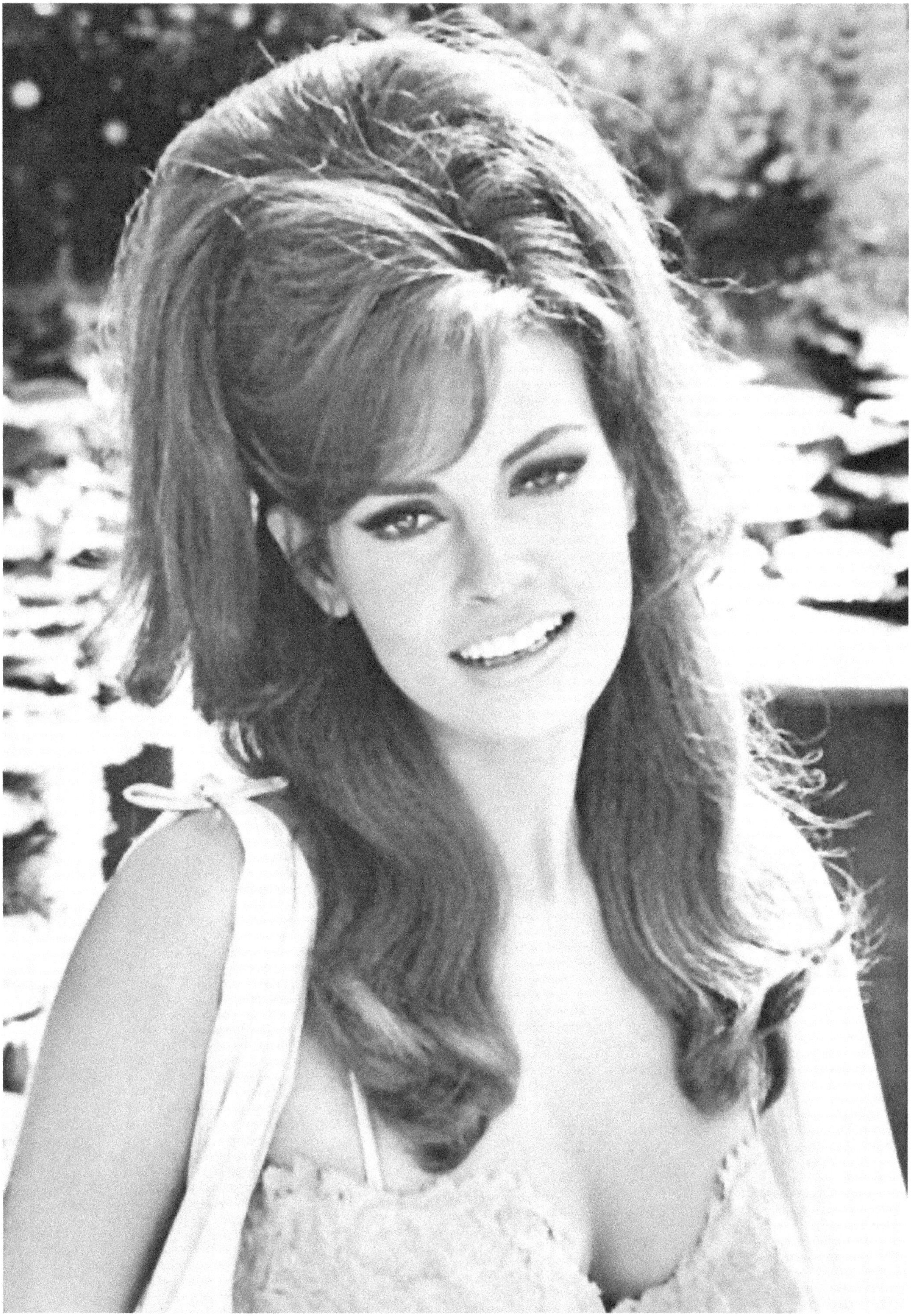

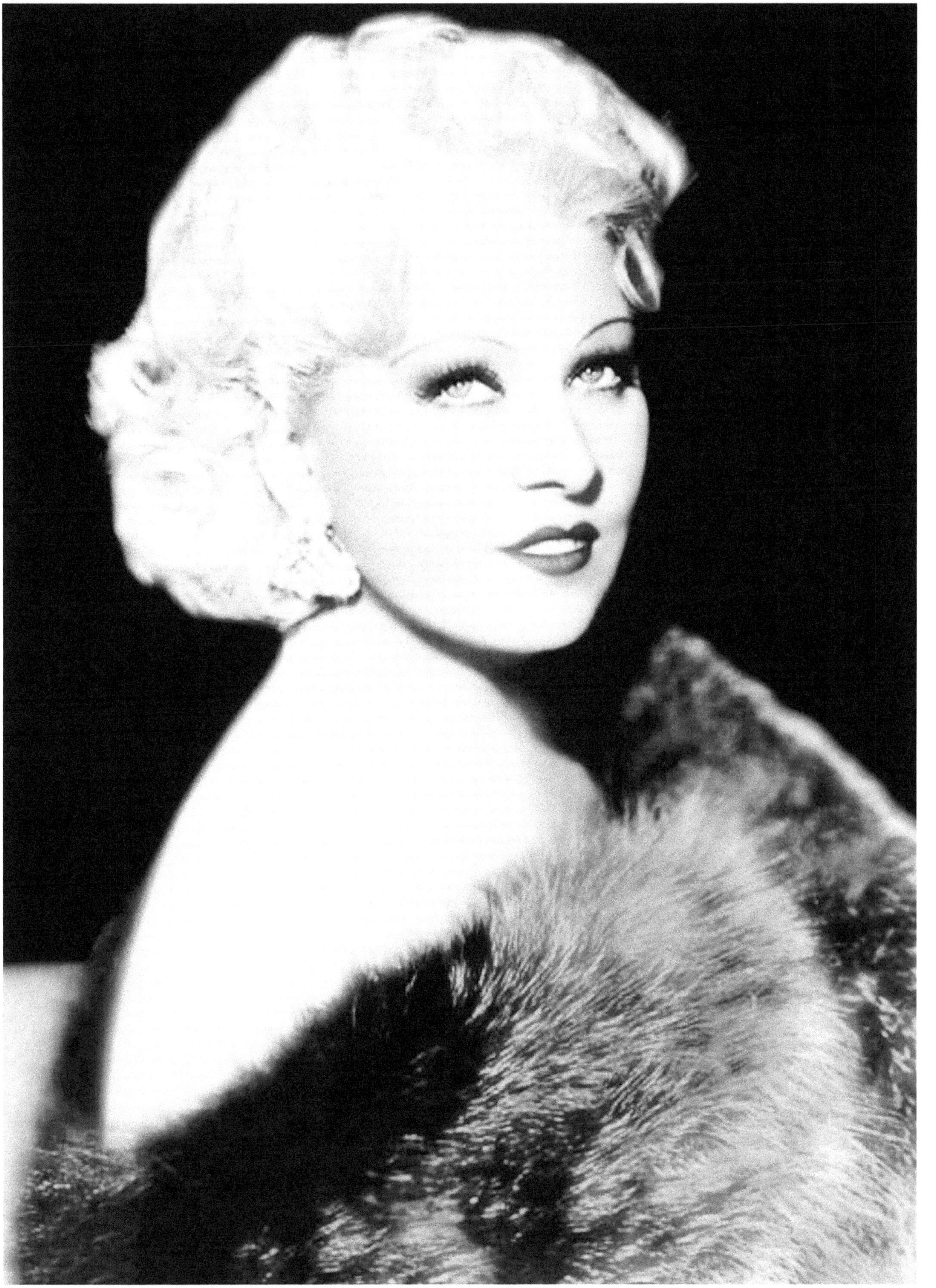

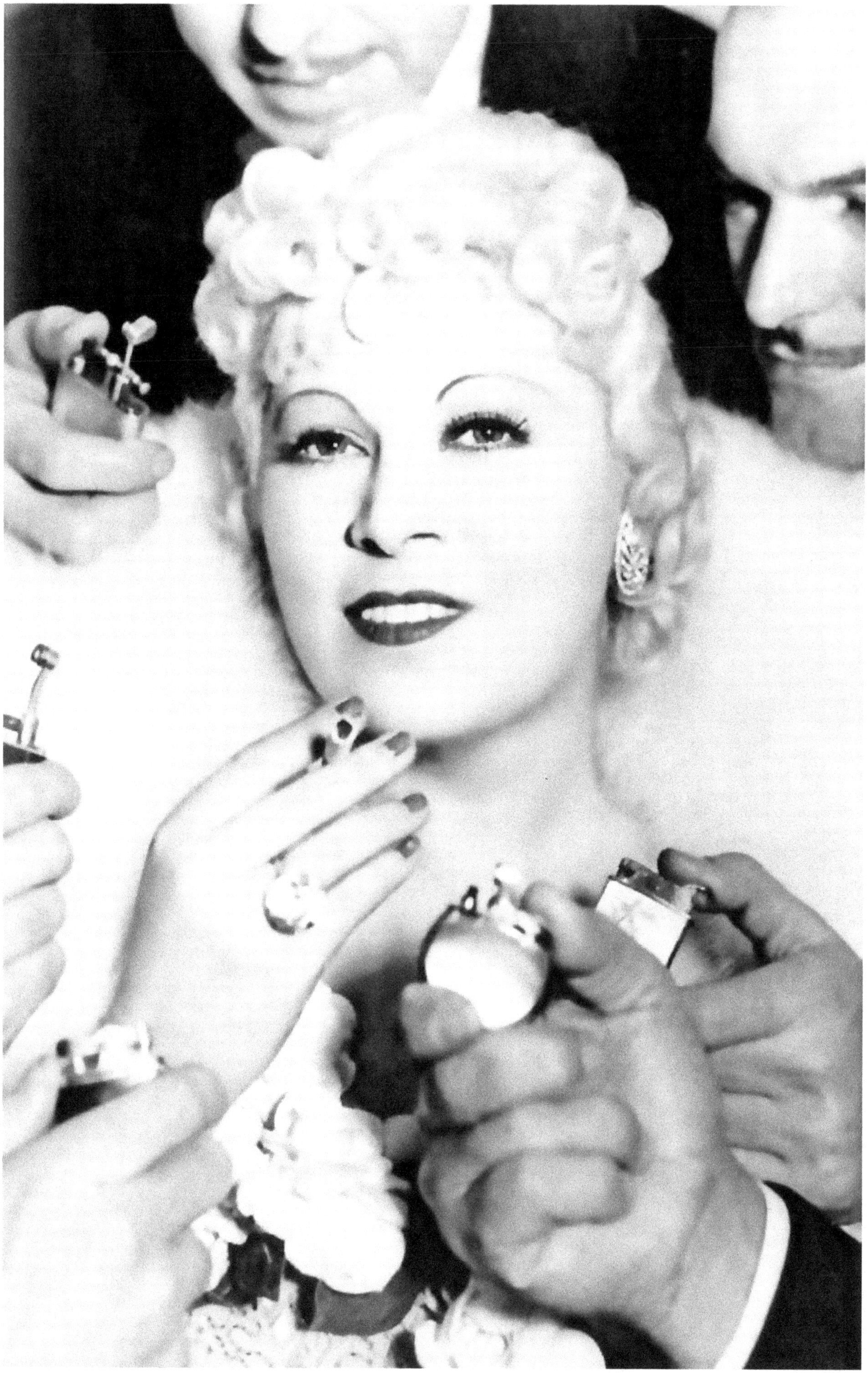

Thank You for Coloring Classic Pin-Ups Grayscale Adult Coloring Book

Compiled by Renee Davenport

Cover Colorist Nina D'aloia

CPSIA information can be obtained
at www.ICGtesting.com
Printed in the USA
LVHW012227270520
656766LV00013B/552